CLIMBING

FOR YOUNG PEOPLE

by Anthony Greenbank

HARRAP LONDON

First published in Great Britain 1977
by GEORGE G. HARRAP & CO LTD
182–184 High Holborn, London WC1V 7AX

ISBN 0 245 53112 2

Photoset in 11 on 12 point Times by
Redwood Burn Limited, Trowbridge & Esher
Printed and bound in Great Britain by
Billing & Sons Limited, Guildford, London and Worcester

CLIMBING

FOR YOUNG PEOPLE

Contents

	Page
1 How to use this Book	6
2 Equipment	9
3 Making Tracks	22
4 Bouldering Experiments	35
5 Learning the Ropes	64
6 Snow Slope Basics	91
7 First Real Climbs	111
Index	128

1 How to use this Book

This book is about CLIMBING – climbing mountains in the safest way possible for ordinary young people. It does not set out to mould you into a boy wonder rock climber or ice climber at this stage of the game; indeed this kind of enthusiast is just as likely to come unstuck when he encounters a type of climbing outside his favourite speciality when still relatively inexperienced. His very aptitude may tempt him to take risks and make decisions which a more experienced climber would see immediately as dangerous. What it does show you, however, is how to complete successfully classic, though by no means desperate, rock climbs; how to scale snow and ice of reasonable difficulty; and how to conduct yourself generally with safety on hills anywhere in the world. Later is the time to specialise if, in fact, you find you prefer one form of the climbing. First, though, you must know the very basic techniques.

Climbing is all about facing problems; the better the problems, the more memorable the climb. Mountains pose such a variety of problems, however, that it takes time for the young climber to experience all the situations which pose risk – even though that climber may show real promise, say, as a cragsman on serious rock faces. There is much more to climbing than cliff-hanging spectacular as it is, however. Hill walking, scrambling, climbing boulders, route planning, navigation, climate control, bivouacking, crossing snow slopes, negotiating ice fields, traversing skylines and adapting to emergencies that may happen on the way and the like are cases in point. In all of these situations, the crux of the matter is the same: how, by knowing what you are about, can you exercise a judgment and competence for each new problem as it arises? This book helps to this end by detailing climbing experiments which, if you practise them carefully, should give you a head start in tackling real climbing difficulties with coolness and purpose, yet which will guide you clear of the rash behaviour so common among young hopefuls prompted by under-preparation and over-ambition.

These experiments will help you find your feet step by step in the safety of your home and neighbourhood. You do, however, require patience, perseverence and application to carry them through. And you must always look on them as being the real thing. Forget about the fact that you may fail time and again in a number of these climbing situations – even when you are only practising them. Instead, give them everything you have to offer just as if your success and safety on 'the hill' were involved (as one day, if the climbing bug really bites, it will).

Begin here. The following experiment proves that you certainly have what it takes in the way of strength – something that many young would-be climbers fear they may lack as they imagine pulling over some rock face overhang on fingertips or holding a falling companion on the rope as he plunges into space: and you need go no further than just outside the house. Try this first climbing experiment and amaze your friends.

Take two towels – large bathtowels are best. Now collect six friends and choose a spot outdoors where the ground is flat and not slippery. Stand straight with your legs apart and feet

positioned firmly. Raise both elbows and clasp your hands in front of the chest, checking your forearms are in a straight line across the upper part of the chest. Ask one friend to hold a towel over and around each elbow and tell them to pull steadily tug-of-war style – *both beginning together*. No matter how hard they try they cannot break your grip. Add another friend to each towel and still the chain will hold even though there are now four people trying to pull your hands apart. The ultimate test is three people to each towel, all pulling together. You hold them all.

Did that surprise you? The fact is that you are a lot stronger than you may think you are. Yet the experiment, like many others in this book, while demanding a certain amount of 'push' (or 'pull' perhaps is the appropriate word here), will do you no harm because the advice is basically sound. Peculiar as it may seem, such experiments are often of direct value. Capers like this, for instance, are common in climbing huts and on camp sites after a day's climbing – along with contests as to who can do the most one-armed pull-ups from beam or branch, who can outpull everyone else using the little fingers only for tug-of-war and who can pick a matchbox up from the floor in their teeth while still holding on to the chair which is supporting them – so your efforts are typical. It is the same with other experiments from learning how to place your hands and feet while rock climbing at ground-level on a brick wall to braking on a steep snow slope while speeding down it on a tea tray. You learn the ropes in the perfect safety of your own backyard, park or field.

But here comes the rub. It is all too easy to become over-confident as you find these experiments do indeed work and your competence at performing them grows. Done as they are in safe surroundings, you gain the impression that this is all there is to it. And a novice in this state of mind cannot wait to try the new techniques out on real mountain slopes and rock faces. To find . . . not just that the higher you go the further there is to fall but also that the colder, the rainier, the windier and the foggier it can so quickly become. And the further you are from help. The change-over from experiments in your backyard laboratory to the testing grounds of the hills therefore needs a strong sense of responsibility and prudence.

This book, I hope, will instil such a sense of reason with which to venture on to all kinds of mountain terrain safely and yet with none of the sense of adventure lacking because of this. Every effort has been made to see that the instructions are clear and simple, but it is highly desirable that a young reader should ask for advice and approval of a responsible adult before attempting any but the simplest experiments. BE CAREFUL, even at this stage.

2 Equipment

Climbing equipment is expensive. The days when hemp ploughcord was used for rope and cut-down macintoshes were worn in the rain are long gone. Fortunately for the novice, however, there is a sharp division between the equipment needed by the expert and that required by the tyro. For the purposes of this book you need only the most basic items as, in fact, are found at home – old clothing and training shoes, for example, and so on. Any climbing ropes and other accessories used for cliffhanging will belong to the person who first takes you climbing – and shows you the ropes with his own as it were. Then, when you have some experience, you too can buy your own.

A newcomer can also take comfort in the fact that when eventually he does need to buy climbing gear, he can follow the example of good climbers and handpick the equipment piece by piece as and when the need arises to add this or that tool to his collection – especially as by then he will already have first-hand experience of other people's gear and will know what he is doing. A climber's equipment, furthermore, is not usually bought in one lump, but is chosen bit by bit in this way. And that means you tend to buy on a self-imposed instalment scheme where the cost is spread over months and the main expense is not shouldered in one go.

EQUIPMENT USED BY CLIMBERS

The climbing accessories you see in use during televised rock face ascents, not to mention those shown in books and newspapers – and which you one day will use – can be listed in a nutshell.

Climbing Boots

Strong uppers cut from one piece of leather sit on top of a thick platform sole with pointed toes. The sole is not only rigid, but is also shod with a Vibram-patterned tread of tough, rubber, rather like a heavy duty truck tyre; it has the same job – to stop you slipping on snow, ice, mud, slush, rock, gravel, scree and so on. Climbing boots look good, rather like ski boots at first glance. They reach high up the ankle. D-rings and hooks carry the laces. They are padded inside like a boxing glove. The tongue is a bellows shape not just a flap. And the uppers come down flush with the welts to present a smooth, streamlined and functional appearance.

Boots

Rock Climbing Shoes

Rock Climbing Shoes

Glove-fitting, featherlight and with pointed toes, 'magic boots' (with names like PAs, EBs, RDs and Masters) are carried in the rucksack to whichever rock face is the target of the day. The climber will then switch his climbing boots for the PAs or whatever – so much better for the delicate footwork on tiny rock wrinkles above. Rock climbing shoes have a stiffened sole of hard smooth rubber like an illegal car tyre which makes walking too painful, but rock climbing a joy.

Clothing
Climbers use the layer system to keep warm in the cold, cool when it's hot and dry during rain. A vest, shirt and several sweaters, for example, will keep the top half of the body warm because 'dead air' is sandwiched between each piece of clothing like the air trapped between the two panes of double glazing windows. As the body grows warmer, layers are stripped off until the body feels comfortable again. Legs, incidentally, are clothed in climbing breeches, a pair of long warm knee-length stockings and, in snow, ice and wet conditions, long gaiters which also reach up to the knee. A woollen hat and warm gloves are also essential.

To keep dry, the layers of clothing are covered with a final layer known as a 'shell'. A nylon cagoule – long smock with pockets and hood – and waterproof over-trousers, tucked inside gaiters, are worn over everything else to keep the climber as dry as possible.

Rucksack

A climber hefts a large bag carried high on the shoulders by comfortable padded straps. It is wedge-shaped, widest at the top, narrower towards the base. Ice axe and crampons are strapped to the outside, a large flap effectively seals the contents from rain. Some sacks, too, have an extendable bivvy sheet inside: you pull out a waterproof lining, then sit inside the lengthened sack if caught out at night on the hill. Unlike rucksacks and pack frames favoured by hikers and ramblers, climbing sacks lack separate pockets – just the one space inside is ideal.

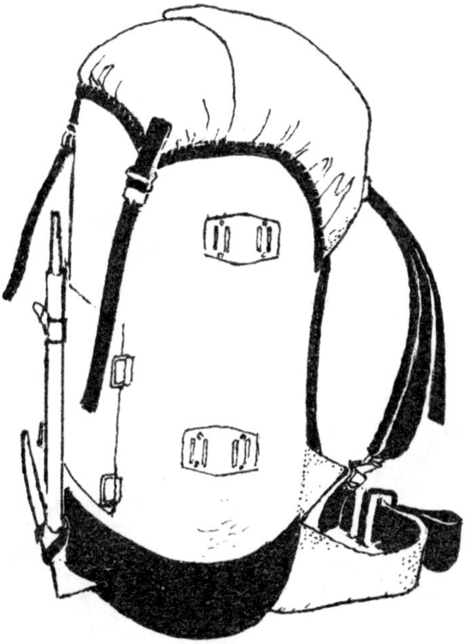

Climber's sack with hip belt to transfer weight through pelvis

Rucksack contents

All climbers should carry the following items: spare sweaters, rations (energy-giving food like nuts, raisins, chocolate, dates, Kendal mint cake, cheese, flapjack and so on); Ordnance Survey 1:50,000 (about one and a quarter inches to a mile) map; Silva compass (to be described later); guidebook for crags to be visited for rock or ice climbing; headtorch which leaves both hands free; whistle; goggles in winter; bivouac bag made from 500 gauge plastic and a last resort if benighted on a mountain (you slide inside the rucksack and extended bivouac sheet – as described above – *inside* the plastic bivouac bag which covers the climber completely); first aid kit.

Ice Axe

This tool is needed for winter walking as well as snow and ice climbing. The handle is short and made from wood, metal or glassfibre – often with an improved rubber fist grip wrapped around its middle. At one end of this is the spike and at the other the axe head with pick and adze. The pick should be 'hooked' to prevent it jumping out when it has been stuck into ice. Beginners are best served with a short tape-sling worn round the wrist so that if they drop the axe it doesn't slide far. The other end of the sling is threaded through the hole in the head of the axe. The axe is often carried in a holster at the waist.

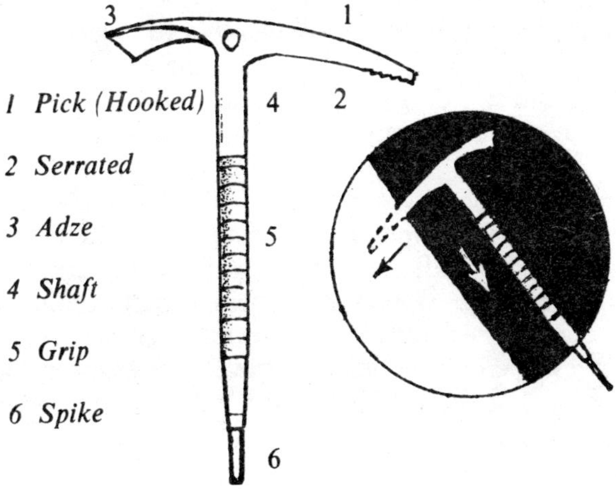

Climbing Helmet

Crash hats are light, comfortable and secure with a chinstrap. They must be strong too, and feel good, like the Ultimate and Joe Brown specification. Glassfibre is the material: it will withstand pebbles and bits of equipment accidentally disloged higher up the rock face which come whirring down and could split a skull. Helmets also keep long hair out of the eyes. And, reckoned by experts as most vital, they can cushion your head in a fall if it bangs against the rock.

Climbing Rope

Cragsmen use a 45 metre (150ft) 11mm rope or, on harder climbs, 90 metres of 9mm rope used double (or two separate 45 metre lengths of 9mm). Perlon rope – technically called 'kern-mantel' – is most popular: long strands of nylon run are bunched inside a braided sheath. But the more old-fashioned three-strand nylon rope – technical name, 'hawser-laid' – is still used, too. Perlon looks best, feels good and is most colourful. Many gear catalogues give full data details.

Your climbing rope, when you do buy one, must be inspected often. Do it foot by foot beneath a strong light. Look for cuts, fraying, burns, grit, oil or anything else which could weaken it. Avoid standing on your rope. Hang it up in a cool dark place out of the sunlight.

Belts and Harnesses

Although the climbing rope can be worn tied around the waist, there are snags if you fall; namely, the rope places great strain on your insides. The Whillans harness which supports the backs of the thighs *and* waist is worn by many climbers on hard routes. However, climbing belts are the choice of many climbing schools for first-time climbers, and are quite adequate for the majority of climbs.

Slings

All climbers carry slings for a variety of purposes: loops of rope varying in diameter from 11mm to 4mm; loops of nylon webbing of varying widths from 2in. to $\frac{5}{8}$in; and small loops of high tensile steel wire. The rope slings are tied with a double fisherman's knot, the nylon webbing slings with the tape knot and the wire slings are swaged. They can be worn, when short, hanging from the climbing belt or harness, or they can be worn directly over the head and shoulder – depending on their length and the climber's preference for 'racking' his slings.

Chocks

Most slings carry a metal chock, commonly called 'nut', threaded on the rope, webbing or wire prior to knotting or splicing the sling into a loop. These chocks – short for chock-stone – can be wedged in narrow cracks and used as anchors in varying ways for belaying climbers to the mountain. They are then lifted out again and recovered by the last climber. Chocks, as shown, are mainly either hexagonally or wedge-shaped. And, they can range from micro size to monsters.

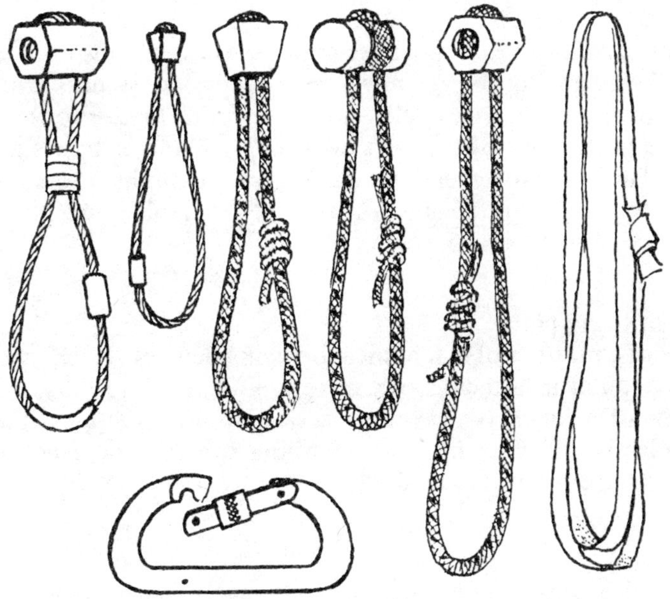

Slings, Chocks and Karabiner

Karabiners

Each sling is used with a karabiner clipped to it, although karabiners may be carried separately from slings – say on a climbing harness or on a bandolier worn across a shoulder guerilla-fashion. A karabiner is an aluminium or steel snap slink with a sprung gate which closes with a comforting 'click!' There are 13mm karabiners, rated at 3,500 kg with a screwgate as shown, and 11mm karabiners rated at 3,000 kg without a screwgate. These are typical of good strong types of karabiner.

Descendeur

The figure of eight alloy device climbers wear dangling from their belt or harness is used for descent. Clipped to the front of the belt or harness, and with two ropes threaded through it, the descendeur allows the climber to slide down the rope in comfort and as fast or as slow as necessary.

Pitons

These metal spikes which are hammered into narrow rock face cracks as anchorage are now largely replaced by nuts which, unlike pitons, leave no ugly scars on the rock face. Pitons have to be beaten out of the rock with many hammer blows after use. They are, however, still used on winter climbs where snow and ice offer limited anchorage and available rock gives a chance of good piton anchorage.

Sticht belay plate

One of a number of mechanical belaying devices, 'Stick' plates are popular as a means of controlling the rope so that in the event of a fall it is braked to a stop smoothly, quickly and painlessly. Only kernmantel climbing rope can be used with this device – not hawser-laid.

Jumars

There are times when a climber may need to climb the rope – after a fall, say, when he may be left swinging in space. Jumars are clamps which, gripped in fist, enables him to climb the rope ratchet-style.

Crampons
Wearing crampons – short spikes strapped snug and tight to the boot soles – allow a climber to move up, down and across snow and ice slopes without having to cut steps with an ice axe. Crampons are light, adjustable and strong. They have 24 sharp points with two points projecting from the toes of each boot at an angle so that the climber can grip steep ice by punching the toes straight into it. Crampons need practise and training in using them effectively. A beginner who uses them before he has mastered snow slopes basics with the ice axe will find them more of a hindrance than a help.

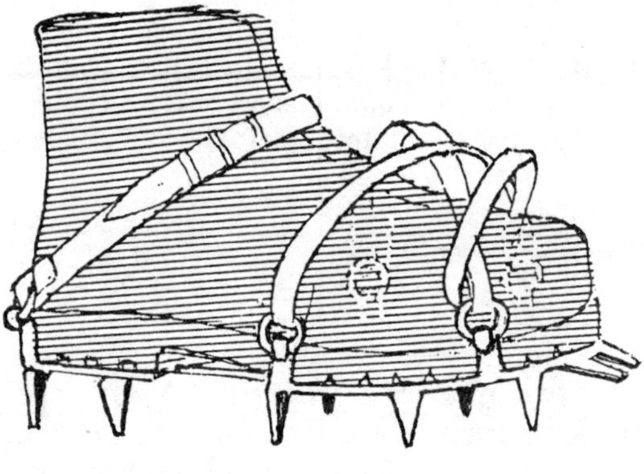

Deadmen
The best anchor for belaying in snow – see Chapter 6 – is the deadman: an alloy plate about a foot square and threaded through the centre with a strong wire sling, it is pushed into a slot cut in the snow. The climber clips himself to the wire sling with a karabiner.

Ice Screws
These are corkscrew-like rods which can either – depending on type – be banged or screwed into the ice for belay anchors. They are recovered by unscrewing.

EQUIPMENT FOR BEGINNERS

Meanwhile, until you are ready to buy your own climbing tackle, the items listed below will be suitable for practising climbing techniques around home. You can, after all, read books and watch climbers climbing and learn quite a lot about equipment that way. Even so, reading and watching aren't the same thing as feeling.

BEGINNER'S GEAR CHECKLIST

Must Buy if Necessary	May Be Found At Home
Boots. Inexpensive boots can be bought with hard rubber (NOT plastic, please) commando soles, D-rings and hooks for lacing, and pointed toes from Army & Navy stores and similar shops. They are not proper climbing boots, but they will do for rough country walking, basic rock climbing and snow slope practise.	*Rock Climbing Shoes.* Pumps, trainers or casual shoes are suitable so long as they can be tightly laced – wear an extra pair of socks if not – and have smooth soles of hard rubber. They must feel snug and good in practise.

(Climbing footwear varies a great deal. Your approach is the main thing. With practise you can adapt to the characteristics of almost any kind of recognised climbing boot or shoe. Even expensive climbing boots can seem too stiff and painful at first until you accept their limitations and set about breaking them in. Do realise this from the start.)

(Two tips for boots: a pair of insides cut from polystyrene tiles will keep your feet warmly insulated. And first-time boot wearers should pack a couple of strips of foam rubber as ankle padding, as they can save a lot of discomfort and often make the boots fit better from the start.)	*Stockings.* Long football stockings are fine. They should not have holes or darns if possible as they lead to blisters on long walks. Cycling stockings are good, too.

Must Buy if Necessary

May Be Found At Home

Trousers. Jeans are OK only for climbing near home or by the roadside, but they are dangerous on hills. They allow body heat to escape too easily when wet. They also bind on the legs making it harder to step high on a cliff in the rain. Thicker wool trousers are warmer for walks on hills and rock climbs – even when wet.

Long Johns. If wearing jeans for roadside climbing or local walking, a pair of pyjama pants worn beneath will make them warmer on cold days.

Leggings. Instead of buying more costly over-trousers as needed on mountains, oilskins or polythene leggings can be carried in case of rain meanwhile.

Gaiters. Cut the feet off a pair of old football stockings. They can be worn over trousers, leggings and the tops of the boots – so keeping small stones out – in bad weather.

(An illustration of the effectiveness of various leg coverings can be seen by taking four 1-gallon metal cans. Dress three of them: one in wool, one in denim and one in wool and cotton inside a polythene bag; leave one bare. Fill all four with hot water of the same temperature. Place all cans in a shaded, windy spot outdoors and record their temperatures each hour. The difference in heat loss is similar to that of a human body.)

Must Buy if Necessary

(A proofed nylon cagoule should be bought as soon as possible for use on hills as it is lighter, more weatherproof and folds into a smaller space in the rucksack.)

(A climber's sack is not really a must until you do become gripped with walks and climbs on hills – then it is.)

Ice Axe. A proper ice axe is a must for winter walking on hills. You don't need an expensive axe as used by experts, detailed earlier, but an ash or hickory-handled ice axe, 75cm long (good average length) and an ordinary carbon steel head with

May Be Found At Home

Vest. A matter of choice. Some climbers never wear one. Others don a tee shirt instead. A wool vest is best.

Shirt. Wool, again, is best. It will stay warm even soaked. And let sweat escape.

Sweaters. Several thin pullovers are more efficient than one or two thick ones. Reason: there are more layers of dead air double glazing the body. Wool is best too because it's warm when wet.

Cagoule. An old raincoat or plastic mac can be cut down if necessary to kneelength. You carry it separately; only to be worn in rain or cold. Cagoules have a hood, but you can substitute this with a hat instead.

Hat. A wool bobble hat or balaclava pulled down over the ears prevents vital body heat escaping in bad weather.

Gloves. Warm woollens best.

Rucksack. An old duffle bag with two padded straps stitched on for the shoulders with a sewing machine will make an inexpensive day sack. Look in your nearest outdoor shop first to check what shoulder straps look like on a modern climber's rucksack.

Must Buy if Necessary

its adze and pick. The pick won't be hooked as on more costly models, but it will be slightly curved and such an axe will see you through the preliminary stages until you need to buy a more specialised ice tool.

Of all the new accessories which have been developed for climbing by tyros in the last decade the climbing helmet is considered by many experts to be the vital aid on rock climbs. Buy a proper one when really hooked.

May Be Found At Home

(Experience on local snow slopes to be detailed in Chapter 7 can be learned with an ice axe improvised from a strong stick. However, this must not be used as the real thing on hills.)

Crash Helmet. A motor cycling or industrial safety helmet will suffice for early rock climbs and snow slope practise (see Chapter 7) even though the person instructing you might not insist on its use. Take one along in any case and wear it.

FINAL REMINDER

The equipment in the right-hand column above is adequate for introductory climbing experience at home. It will also, so long as you are not proud (and many great climbers have begun their mountain career with similar unsophisticated tackle), be suitable for preliminary rock face and snow slope excursions in company with an experienced climber who has all the accoutrements of ropes and slings, etcetera. But the gear in the left-hand column *is* necessary because it has been proved safe for most people on most mountain routes most of the time . . . Yes, when actual hills are involved rather than playgrounds much nearer to home.

By the time you are ready to buy your own gear you will have seen and handled similar equipment. You will have a much better idea what climbing is about. By visiting various climbing shops and devouring their catalogues – some are as comprehensive and easy-to-read as instructional books on climbing – you will know just the items you do need. And so you spend your money a lot more wisely than you would if you were to rush off to the nearest mountain shop now.

3 Making Tracks

This book is about climbing rather than walking. You can reach many mountain tops by walking without meeting any rock, snow or ice climbing whatsoever, but this does not make you a 'climber'. Climbing, however, does include a great deal of walking along tracks to reach high crags, ice climbs and mountain crest traverses – not to mention the tramping necessary to get you to the foot of the mountain in the first place. Even now, when possibly you are still too young to go rambling in local countryside without an older person going too, walking plays its part. You should, for instance, make tracks if at all possible to watch climbers actually climbing, and you should also visit the big mountains to see if they really haunt you as much as you thought they would on close acquaintance. It is far better to be prompted to climb through that yearning for high places the real climber feels after seeing mountains at first hand for the first time – even when lashed with rain and hooded with mist – than taking up climbing because it is an O.K. thing to do. Making tracks like this is the beginning, done the correct way, to mountain safety as long as you climb.

MAKE A CLIMBING QUEST

Make tracks to your public library to discover the nearest rock face to your home as well as the most readily-reached mountains. One book in particular – E. C. Pyatt's *Where to climb in the British Isles* – will show the scope for 'local' crags and there are good books on Snowdonia, the Lake District and Scottish Highlands. While your nearest rock face will most likely be easily reached by bus or car and be near the roadside, Ogwen, Wasdale, Glencoe – great mountain valleys all – or wherever will in all probability be a weekend's trip involving train, coach or car and at least one night camping or youth hostelling among the hills.

Visit the local crag on a fine Saturday or Sunday afternoon. Any popular outcrop like Stannage near Sheffield or Harrison's near London will swarm with climbers on the many different routes – a great opportunity to study equipment, technique and style. And to listen to what is going on all around you. Don't be tempted, though, to try easy-looking short climbs on your own – they will often prove tougher than they look. Don't pester climbers either, but take a camera (the cheapest cartridge-loading model will still take good snaps of cragsmen in action) and casually chat up climbers not actually climbing as you take various shots. Climbers are an informal, friendly lot and easy to talk with if they see you are keen without being intense about it. Meanwhile all that climbing is taking place in front of the lens – exactly as it would thousands of feet up a cliff perched high on a mountain.

(Tips for 'shooting' climbers: shoot across the face at climber silhouetted against the sky; expose for shadows; use fastest speed; shoot when climber is engrossed in moving up first few feet of a climb – just missing out the ground for the picture.)

As for visiting North Wales, the Lakes or Scotland . . . Make tracks for the valleys flanked by the highest mountains and, depending on your age and limitations, plan accordingly. If you are still a ten-year-old or thereabouts you will need to go with parents or someone older, but no bother there so long as you all know the score. Namely, that unless they are climbers themselves and the circumstances are right, you undertake only the easiest excursions whether a walk around a lake hemmed in by those towering slopes or over an easy pass which crosses from one valley to another and where you are always conscious of the jagged skyline high above which you know you will reach some other day. Apart from being safer, you – and especially you – are not put off the hills for life by a walk which was much too strenuous for young legs.

If, however, you are old enough to make tracks for the mountains with friends of your own age then these initial easy mountain expeditions by which you make your first acquaintance with hills must allow for the following factors.

THE GOLDEN RULES OF MOUNTAIN SAFETY

Any high, remote and exposed ground, even moorland in Devon or Derbyshire, can be dangerous whatever the time of year. The higher you climb, the more the weather intensifies and what may have been a mild valley breeze can become a piercing icy wind at 500 feet which is Arctic in its threat. Temperatures drop rapidly too, wind speeds increase, rain becomes torrential and there is danger from fast-moving mists and low cloud which suddenly reduce visibility to a few feet. For those who disregard the basic safety precautions, the onset of bad weather can mean acute physical discomfort, loss of direction, growing fear and exhaustion and even collapse – a victim of hypothermia (see *Survival for Young People*).

The higher you go the more rugged becomes the terrain too. Routes cross boulder slopes, slippery rocks, thick heather and bracken slopes which conceal holes and loose stones where it is only too easy to twist an ankle. Should you lose the path progress becomes slow and you need extra care and physical effort which, affected by the increasingly poorer weather, present real risk. The following mountain safety rules, however, will help you to make a safe return – so long as you make a conscientious effort to stick to them.

Your group of friends

Even the easiest walk among mountains is all the safer if there are four of you. Any smaller group poses problems if, say, a person is injured and someone has to go for help. With four people, one stays with the casualty and the other two act as 'runners' to the nearest farm or telephone, but with a smaller group it's not as simple nor as safe . . . As for one person on their own – they are really vulnerable even when experienced.

A leader should be chosen before starting out: someone who is level-headed and has the respect of the others, whatever mutual mickey-taking passes between you. An older, stronger person is the ideal on early hill forays and your parents may well decide it could be themselves.

The leader's aim should be to set a slow pace, then to keep the group together and avoid, at all costs, splitting it – possibly through arguments caused by fatigue or laziness. He should see the slow walkers are not left behind, and that the strong walkers don't race on ahead. When one person stops – to tie a boot lace, say – everyone else should stop or large gaps develop between the members of the group. And if someone is tiring fast, they should go to the front where walking is easier.

The leader must take decisions, too, after everyone else has had their say. This means the rest of the party are freed of the responsibilities which goes into making a decision and can each concentrate on playing their own part. As you grow more experienced in mountains, however, the need for a leader and his reminders grows far less.

Wear boots

Boots fitted with a rubber mountaineering sole as outlined in Chapter 2 are necessary on hills. Unfortunately new boots can blister the feet all too easily. Be ready by carrying stretch fabric dressing strip and a pair of scissors in case you feel the boots beginning to rub. If you know for sure the boots are uncomfortable, however, stick lengths of the dressing strip over the heels and around each toe before you even set out. It's an unconventional treatment which works (football players use it).

Take along warm clothing

Already stressed in Chapter 2, 'taking along' warm clothing does NOT mean 'wearing' it unless you are feeling cold. The chances are, however, your body will warm up so quickly – even on a cold, dry day. After ten minutes or so walking uphill, you will be only too glad to stash the anorak or cagoule and most sweaters back in the rucksack. However, you should still take sweaters and waterproofs along in the warmest weather just in case conditions change. But keep them in the rucksack from the start as padding for your back against hard objects so that, in fact, your rucksack feels like a neat and lightweight punchbag resting on your back.

Take along reserve rations

A hot drink in a vacuum flask is a great reviver. So are chocolate, mint cake, nuts, raisins, glucose tablets and flapjack. To make survival biscuits take: 3 cups oatmeal or cornflakes, 2½ cups powdered milk, 1 cup white sugar, 3 tablespoons honey, 3 tbs water, $\frac{1}{2}$ package of citrus flavoured gelatin, $\frac{1}{4}$ tsp salt. Place all dry ingredients except gelatin in mixing bowl; combine honey and water and bring to boil; dissolve the gelatin in this mixture, then add the dry ingredients: mix well; add water a teaspoon at a time until the mixture is moist enough to press into two bars of 'toffee'. Place in an oven and dry under a very low heat. Wrap in foil and they will keep indefinitely.

Take survival aids

A pea whistle, flashlight and small first-aid kit are sensible back-up supplies for introductory mountain walks. (For details on how to use them read *Survival for Young People.*)

Take map & compass

The Silva compass – like the Swiss Army penknife – is a tool specially suited to mountaineering. So are the new Ordnance Survey 1:50,000 maps which are near an inch and a quarter to the mile in scale – so crisp and clear in detail that the landscape clicks into a three-dimensional picture at a glance. Only the young climber must be able to use these necessary aids from the beginning – owning them is not enough. You may, for instance, be among a group led by an experienced climber, but should the party become separated through unforseen circumstances, each person must then be able to find their way through thick mist to the valley and safety.

Make a silver arrow compass

You can make a Silva-type compass from any ordinary compass where a magnetic needle is simply mounted over a card bearing the degrees of the compass from 0°–360°, a thick piece of cardboard; some silver foil; and a little hard gloss enamel paint. Cut the cardboard to shape as shown, then slice out the hole through it with a lino knife so the compass fits tightly into this space. Paint the cardboard with enamel and fix an arrow cut from the foil exactly as in the position illustrated. This imitation of a Silva compass is much more accurate than the ordinary compass was on its own. It will guide you across local countryside like radar through thick mist or pitch darkness.

Draw a rough map of a nearby field or local park. But use the compass to help you as all real maps are drawn with north at the top. So place the compass on the blank paper on a flat surface. Turn the paper (compass on it) until the needle hovers over 'N'. (Disregard the silver foil Direction of Travel arrow for now.) Now face that way and sketch the map from this

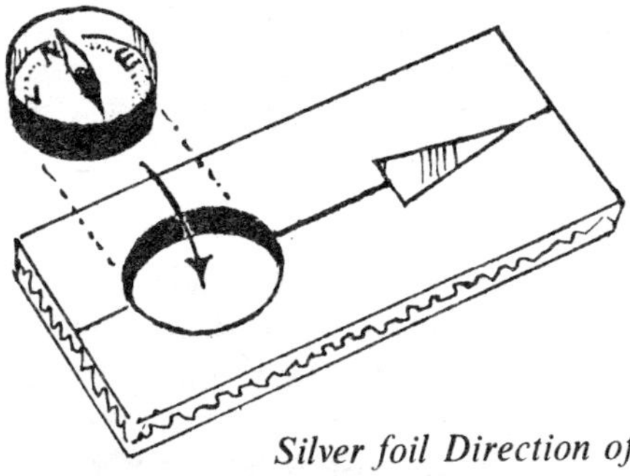

Silver foil Direction of Travel arrow

angle. The northern countryside will be at the top. Wait until dark. Then go out with a friend. Take a flashlight, the map and compass. And go to one specific point marked on your map – a tree or rock, say.

Spread the map on the grass and put the compass on top so that the north-to-south line is parallel with the paper's edge, with 'N' at top. (The magnetic needle itself need not point to north.) Now decide where you want to walk – say a far corner of the field or park. Hold the compass housing perfectly steady – north-to-south line pointing up and down the map – and turn the cardboard plate until one edge is touching the point where you are (let's call it 'A'), and the point where you wish to reach, 'B'. Make sure everything is firm. Check the number of degrees on the compass card which now nudges the end of the Direction of Travel arrow, then lift the compass from the map. Now head across country holding the compass so the needle points to north. You, however, follow the silver D.O.T. arrow at the setting you worked out on the map. (Say your direction was due east, it would be 'E' or 90°.) And you can put the map away. (BUT remember that any metal near the needle – belt buckle, metal watch strap or whatever – may pull it off course and give you a false reading.)

How to keep dead on course

Stand compass in hand, keeping the needle over 'N'. Send your friend in the direction you are heading. Tell him to stop while he is still within your flashlight's beam. Then walk up to him – and, consulting your compass, send him on his way again. Go on repeating this – it is one way in which you can keep a straight line along a bearing in bad visibility. If you have a second friend to help, this method is all the more accurate as you can then space out two people ahead in line with your D.O.T. arrow.

Note concerning Ordnance Survey maps

As Ordnance Survey maps are drawn to true north there is a difference from your hand-drawn map. Because the magnetic north pole (which moves about inside the Arctic Circle) drags the needle to west or east of true north depending on the region (in Britain it is to the west); always allow for this deflection. So, wherever you take a bearing in the way described above from an Ordnance Survey map, add 8° or whatever the magnetic difference is to the number of degrees actually resting against the D.O.T. arrow. As the magnetic north pole strays from district to district the Ordnance Survey maps bear a diagram and a formula on each sheet (among the key to the map symbols) which gives the local magnetic variant. This magnetic variation is, of course, most up to date on the latest maps. Do check this; it varies through Britain.

DANGERS OF BEARINGS

Pocket your home-made precision compass now and take random bearings whenever you have a moment – drawing a rough map of the room, backyard or wherever you happen to be. Then work out different bearings, and walk along them following the D.O.T. arrow to see if you can, in fact, arrive at your destination looking down at the floor and never towards where you hope your bearing will lead. It quickly becomes obvious that bearings always take the shortest line between two points. And that on mountains this could be highly dangerous – cutting across cliffs, steep slopes, ravines, lakes and other hazards. In such cases more than one bearing must be used, and each leg of the trip through mist must be timed so that you know when to take a fresh bearing on to the next leg. It is important to know therefore more about route planning before you start. It is hardly ever straight-line planning.

Plan walks carefully

Go over the map first with a toothcomb. Work out exactly where you are going to walk – even on the easiest preliminary walks. You must allow enough time to get back well within darkness, and not overestimate your physical ability.

If undertaking the easiest walks first gives an idea of the effort involved, it helps you to learn planning them, too. Use a piece of string to determine how many inches the walk is to be on the map – even a low-level tour around a lake could prove too long because of the sheer distance involved. Then think in miles. On mountains, however, there is the height to climb to take into consideration as well and this calls for a greater expenditure of effort and longer time necessary.

In the margins of the map is given the scale so that you can convert those inches into miles – and also the spacing of the contour lines which represent height on the map. There is usually 50 feet between each contour line with an extra thick contour line every 250 feet. The diagram overleaf shows a simple example of how contours break down the height of hills – as if you cut a potato or turnip in half and then slice one of the halves at intervals of a centimetre. That's your hill neatly contoured. From a side view it looks like (1). But from the top it looks like (2). And it's this view which forms a network of contours on a map. (Although 1:50,000 map contours are given to the nearest metre, the height you climb can still be measured in feet because the vertical interval between contours is 50 feet.)

As you see, contours close together mean steep hillsides; far apart, they indicate gentle slopes. There are also other contour formations which show ridges, valleys, spurs containing valleys, mountain passes and solitary shoulders leading to the summit of a peak.

Now, knowing the number of miles to be walked, and by totting up the contours for height to be climbed (height dropped is ignored) you can work out a very approximate speed guide. Thus, you walk at 3 m.p.h. plus half an hour for every 1,000 feet climbed. This formula – known as Naismith's rule – takes into account short rests, but that is all. It is also based on the 'normal' conditions of a calm, fine day. However. . . .

Bearing in mind the contours of the mountains immediately around your planned walk, it helps to check your route according to the following principles. Naismith's rule, rough

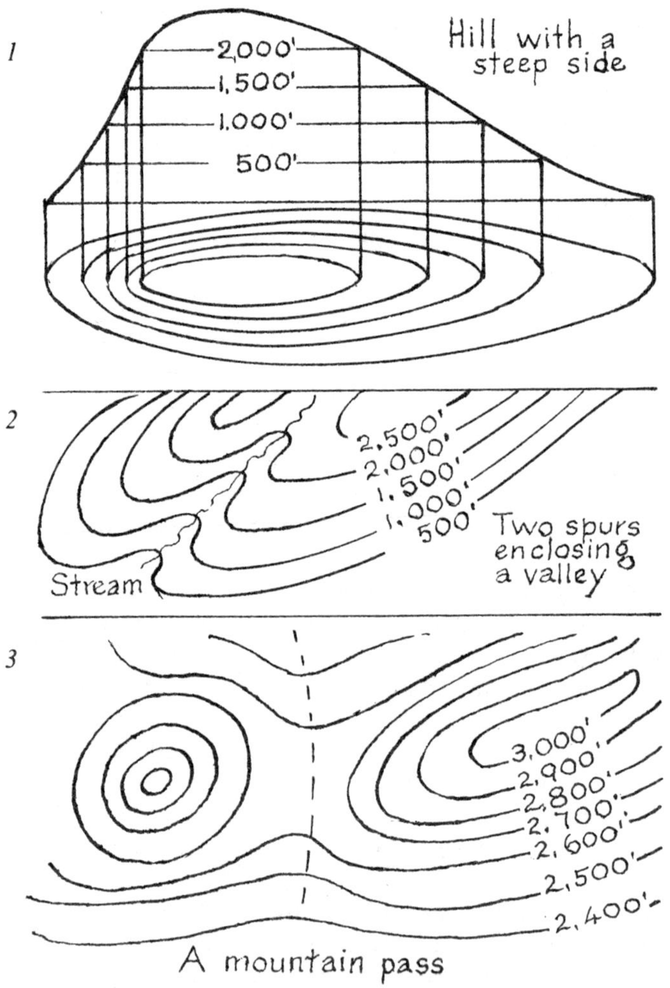

guide as it is, is still a basis in working out the times you can expect to reach a list of places (as landmarks) along your tracks. As your experience grows you will find that not only may you have to amend the rule which is proving too speedy for you – say you are happiest at an approximate speed of 2½ m.p.h. and it takes you an hour to climb 1,500 feet – but you will also have to adjust your 'Route List' times when conditions overhead and underfoot are bad, and you are recovering from a cold and the rucksack is weightier than normal!

Your 'Route List' should be roughed out on a plain postcard as below, and the reverse side should contain details of 'escape routes'.

FROM	TO	DISTANCE	HEIGHT CLIMBED	COMPASS BEARINGS IN CASE OF MIST	TIME
		MILES	FT	← TOTAL →	HRS

P.T.O for reverse side of card

ESCAPE ROUTES
WRITE DOWN DETAILS OF EASY WAYS OFF HIGH GROUND IN CASE OF SUDDEN CHANGES OF WEATHER. COMPASS BEARINGS FROM CERTAIN OBVIOUS LANDMARKS ARE A HELP

LOOK FOR

Paths. Many mountain tracks are not shown on the map, but do use those you find heading in your direction. Cairns – piles of rocks – signpost the way along many mountain tracks.

Easy slopes. If you must leave a path to climb or descend choose where the contours are well spaced rather than attack steep grass, rocks and scree on close-packed contours.

Ridges. The best walking always lies along the skyline where the main height has been gained, and now there is less distance to climb on the ups and downs of a horizon's crest. The footing is often short turf and the views are fantastic. The best ridges for beginners are those about 500–700 feet high, low enough to be safe, yet looking into the heart of higher mountains across the way and so set your heart beating for the real thing. But do them in fine weather at first.

(Never overlook the power of wind when high – even at 500 feet. It can not only chill you, but blow you over and make you trip by filling your eyes with tears.)

AVOID AVOID

'Contouring' means walking across a hillside rather than climbing upwards. It is a strain on the ankles and should be avoided unless you are on a path.

Cliffs. Rock faces anywhere near your route must be given a wide berth. Be aware of them even on popular tracks: they can be real traps in mist. They are shown on maps with 'hachures'. Always check your route for hachures in the vicinity in case of bad weather.

Scree. This rock face rubble covers mountainsides with acres of loose stones. To the expert it is a quick way down; to the tyro it is a frequent cause of accidents. Avoid scree and grass slopes until you have more experience.

Streams/Bogs/Gullies. Avoid streams because water takes the fast way downhill and often falls down risky ravines; bogs slow you down; steep rifts – gullies – in cliffs and hillsides contain sudden drops and treacherously loose rock.

Steep Grass. You can rocket down steep wet grass like a dive-bomber when wearing waterproofs. The same goes for heather. Steep dry grass can be just as risky in summer if you slip; it can be worse than ice, for ice is obvious.

Snow & Ice. Keep clear of winter conditions on hills until you have first learned to use an ice axe and rope competently, even for winter hill walks. Until then, keep to valley bottom trips.

Check weather forecasts

Newspapers and the radio will keep you up to date. You can also phone the Met Office (number in the phone book). Keep a constant look out for changes. On high ground, mist and rain can close in with frightening speed.

Turn back if . . .

Never hesitate to turn back or cut a walk short if the weather deteriorates or if a route is proving too much for a companion or for the group. It can take a lot more courage to turn back at times than to press on, but there can be disastrous consequences if you do keep going. Don't be afraid to admit it.

Stay together

Whatever happens – unless, say, someone has an accident and one person must stay with them while the others go for help – you stay together as a group. All walking slowly and in single file uphill, and all accepting the decisions of the group leader. A tip here: the best pace which keeps a group together is the one where you can all talk to each other without feeling out of breath as you step uphill. If you can't do this comfortably – you are all travelling too fast and the front person should slow down.

Always leave word

Always leave word where you are going and when you expect to return. Tell the people at the place where you are staying, or leave a note on the seat of your car or on a tent pole. A search party has far less chance of finding you unless they have some idea where you are. And do report your return to those expecting you.

Keep to your planned route . . .

If for some reason you have to spend the night in some other accommodation rather than return to base, telephone either the place where you were staying or the police. Tell them what has happened – and promptly. Failure to do this may mean search parties spending many wasted hours looking for you.

Know what to do in an emergency

There are three excellent books on this subject on sale at climbing shops, and you can order them from book shops. *Safety on Mountains* (The Sports Council), *The Mountain Rescue Handbook* (Mountain Rescue Committee), *Mountain Leadership* (Eric Langmuir for Scottish Sports Council). There is also *Survival for Young People.* Read them and you will know what to do in cases of accident, illness or being overtaken by bad weather or darkness.

Expect the worst

Look on bad weather as normal for British hills, and good weather as the exception. Then be pleasantly surprised when conditions turn out to be good after all. If you follow this rule encountering bad weather is never 'bad luck' – the only luck, in fact, is the 'good luck' when it's fine. To this end, see that you have good equipment and clothing that has been proved safe for mountains. It is a sobering thought that instructors at Glenmore Lodge – the Scottish Sports Council outdoor centre near Aviemore in the Cairngorms – accept wearing TWO anoraks on top of everything else as normal attire, so Arctic is the weather at times.

4 Bouldering Experiments

Boulder problems are, as you might imagine, climbs in miniature – but on 'boulders' rather than on rock faces. And bouldering is the art of overcoming such climbing difficulties – difficulties which would pose a psychologically much more serious problem high on a cliff – at ground-level. Rock climbing, being one of the aspects of mountaineering where it is necessary to be on your toes all the time, moreover, requires as much bouldering practise as the young climber can possibly manage; you simply can't have enough of it say good climbers who go to some pains – sometimes barking shins and grazing elbows – practising what they preach.

Although a few minor cuts and bruises can be expected bouldering, nothing worse ever happens because you are climbing so near to the ground. Indeed the kind of bouldering detailed here will ensure you are not usually more than four feet above it and never more than a height of more than twice *your* height – and then with an extra soft landing below at that. Yet the beauty of bouldering is you can really stretch yourself to the limit trying the one particular problem which seems impossible again and again until you eventually climb it successfully. Such persistence means you become increasingly proficient – so long as you continue to practise. And practise hard.

This is a chapter of climbing experiments. To stop it becoming a chapter of accidents, however, do ask friends to accompany your early bouldering attempts even if they have no lasting interest in climbing. And – as well as being friends – they should be older, responsible people, too. The idea is that others can stand by you and help you down if stuck or prevent you overbalancing too drastically if you fall, and you can do the same for them. As for potential knocks while bouldering, remember that if adventure is taken out of life too early, so that it holds no more risk than flying paper darts, you can't benefit.

You tend to learn more from living a little precariously at times and, in fact, from seeing the consequences of going too far at ground-level. It is, after all, only by contact with, and in imitation of, the real world – in this case the climbing world – that an adult sense of responsibility and danger emerges later. So go to it, but go accompanied. Besides, the sound of others encouraging (and barracking!) helps a lot too.

IT MUST BE STRESSED AGAIN, HOWEVER, THAT THE BOULDER PROBLEMS YOU DISCOVER AT HOME MUST MAINLY BE TRAVERSES WHERE YOU CLIMB A FOOT OR TWO UPWARDS (NEVER MORE THAN FOUR FEET) AND THEN STEP OUT ACROSS TO RIGHT OR LEFT. THE AIM BEING THEN TO CONTINUE MORE OR LESS AT THAT LEVEL FROM FOOTHOLD TO FOOTHOLD AND FROM HANDHOLD TO HANDHOLD UNTIL YOU HAVE CLIMBED ACROSS ALL THE DIFFICULTIES AND REACHED THE FAR SIDE WITHOUT FALLING OFF. FOR THOSE OTHER EXPERIMENTS WHICH ARE THE EXCEPTION, BECAUSE IT IS NECESSARY TO CLIMB UPWARDS ALL THE WAY RATHER THAN TRAVERSE FROM SIDE TO SIDE, THE TOTAL HEIGHT OF THE BOULDER PROBLEM INVOLVED SHOULD NEVER BE MORE THAN TWICE YOUR OWN HEIGHT AND GREAT CARE SHOULD BE TAKEN TO SEE THE LANDING BELOW IS SOFT.

TRY A TERRIBLE TRAVERSE AT HOME

Inside your cellar, attic, boxroom, garage, backyard or garden – or anywhere with space around the walls – is scope for a dummy traversing run. Simply place objects like building bricks, books, boxes and wooden chairs at intervals around and touching the walls and arrange each so the distance in between these 'footholds' is a good stride apart. The idea is to make your way around all the walls from foothold to foothold – sometimes stepping from, say, a book to a brick, from that brick up on to a chair, then down to a book, then on to another book, across to a stool then on to a box, down to a brick and so on. As you do this, press both hands flat against the wall because for this experiment you are not trying to find handholds but are concentrating on basic footsteps from hold to hold without overbalancing and touching the floor. Even at this elementary stage, however, you begin to appreciate the problems facing a climber. Here is just one example.

CRACK A SHOE POLISH TIN CRUX

The 'crux' is the hardest part of a rock climb and during your circumnavigation of the room you should incorporate at least one such 'desperate' move. In this case it is one foothold which is much smaller than the others – an old shoe polish tin full of sand or coins to prevent it skidding on the floor. Place it between two bricks or heavy books at the full limit of your stride between each foothold.

When such an impasse is reached on a real traverse high on a rock face the climber is faced with a choice of ways with which to tackle the problem; the snag being that while each book or brick-sized hold will accommodate both feet you can only land one foot at a time on the shoe polish tin. And this can mean your legs can get into an awful tangle if you go about it the wrong way. Practise the following two methods, though, and the principles involved – one of crossing your legs the *correct* way; the other of changing feet on a small foothold – will always stand you in good stead.

The first method is called 'putting a foot through'. Imagine you are standing two-footed on the book or brick to the right of the shoe polish tin, and your aim is to be able to stand two-footed on the brick or book at the far side of that tin. Balance on the left foot at the left end of your present foothold, therefore, press both hands flat against the wall and step 'through' with the right foot until by really stretching out with that leg you can plant the right toes on the tin, angling the shoe to point towards the wall. Transfer your weight on to the right leg, stand straight on the tin and step across once more but now with the left leg on to the book or brick on the far side. Bring both shoes together on top of it and you have cracked your first crux.

The changing feet method is also simple, but needs more practise to do it deftly. (And if you do it clumsily on a real climb you could miss and fall off!). Step left-footed on to the shoe polish tin, press both hands hard on the wall – not holding on to anything – and with a skip swap feet on the tin, striding left with the left as right foot hits tin, then follows left on to book. And that's all there is to it. Once you have learned not to miss the tin as you jump you are ready for rather more serious stuff . . .

But don't forget these two tricks. Doing one or the other can often solve a climbing problem which was proving impossible and not only on traverses either, but on pieces of climbing directly upwards too.

FIND THE BOULDERS ON YOUR DOORSTEP

Rock climbing movements don't have to be practised on actual rock boulders. If you are fortunate enough to live near such cameo cliffs, of course, you can make full use of them for early traversing attempts. For many young climbers, however, more mundane climbing surfaces will have to suffice. Used properly, though, they offer many more exciting possibilities than may first appear.

Here, then, is a list of potential boulder problems, and how to prepare them for the time when you first try finding your feet on the difficulties they offer.

BRICK OR STONE WALLS

Look for walls where low climbing traverses are allowed. Examples are walls in parks or inside the grounds of a school, perhaps the wall of your garden, garage or even the house itself. Then there are walls of old buildings like warehouses and barns not to mention the marvellous climbing along canals, wharves, crumbling old bridges and railway embankments where trains no longer run. Another excellent choice – often set back at a steep angle – is the wall below the promenade at the seaside – it has all the ruggedness of a disused railway embankment and you land on sand if forced to jump from a low-level traverse. As you are never going to be far from the deck on any of these walls, in fact, they are really safe for training purposes.

Now you may not yet realise this fact of life, but there are other people who always take the opposite view. Inspectors, guards and policemen are just as likely to come along and shunt you off even though you know the precautions you are taking as detailed here are essentially safe. The only advice I can give is: have a good look round for boulder problems that are free from any kind of restriction and use them well. The fact that you are only climbing in a hedgehopping manner is an advantage here, anyway, as it is nowhere near as obvious from a distance that you are climbing at all as it would be if you were making direct ascents for quite a height. All the more reason then to keep low in training.

Having found a good wall, therefore, check it for certain hazards.

Drainpipes

Avoid climbing up drainpipes. In fact, avoid using them as footholds or handholds at all as pulling on them will weaken them. If it is necessary to stride past a drainpipe on a low-level traverse such a huge handhold should be looked on as illegal; it makes the climbing too easy. Touch the pipe and pay the penalty. You go back to the start of the traverse and begin again.

Porches

Leave porches alone as these too can be weakened by hard pulling.

Window sills

Ban the assistance of window sills where these ledges offer large handholds across a traverse and make the climbing too simple. Make it a rule that to touch a sill is cheating and to do so means the offender has to jump down and start all over again. Where you find a window sill at a level of slightly more than your height with arms raised, however, and where it is set into a wall where climbing is allowed it can be put to a different purpose – practising the mantelshelf move described later in this chapter.

Doorways

Several kinds of climbing movement can be practised across and up inside a doorway as we shall presently see. And a doorway occurring mid-way along a low traverse can prove a crux which will give the young climber pause for thought, for he must cross the gap without touching the ground.

Passages and corridors

Chimneying and bridging techniques which follow later in the chapter can be practised in literally a wide variety of ways when the walls are no more than three feet apart or even closer – better for shorter legs and arms.

TREES

Not only can climbing trees prove dangerous because branches sometimes break without warning, there is no real value either in reaching for and grasping the large handholds they have to offer. Bouldering is, after all, about learning how to use the smallest toe-holds and fingerholds while you have the chance to practise in safe surroundings and at leisure. In one respect, however, trees can provide useful practise: if you select those with the largest trunks and climb around them, say at around the four-foot mark from the ground, you can aim to finish back at the point from where you began without touching the ground – ideal practise and known as a 'girdle traverse'.

The more massive the trunk therefore the better the boulder problems challenging you. Bark which splits, flakes or peels is useless, of course, compared with the tree surface which remains compact as you push and pull against the cracks seaming it. And – as we shall see – the forks between trunks and branches can also give great practise too.

ROCKS

Large boulders and small rock outcrops in the vicinity might be found in a park, on a beach, against a hill, among trees – the possibilities are varied. Houses are sometimes built on a bedrock which thrusts through the ground and which might offer several climbing movements in your garden. Sea cliffs and old quarries can also be used for low-level traverses so long as they are low-level and not diagonal or direct ascents up such obviously dangerous places. You never know when rock peeps through the earth, and the fact that you may live in a lowland area does not mean there is no chance of finding rock nearby somewhere; keep your eyes open and you might be surprised.

CLIMBING WALLS

There are more than 300 climbing walls at schools, colleges and sports centres throughout Britain. Built as rock face replicas to provide the novice with experience and the experienced with training, they are serious challenges in most cases and you need a safety rope from above while you climb them. Also you have to be 16 or supervised, and you reach up at your own risk. But low-level traverses are still possible if there are climbing walls in your locality where it is possible to practise. But remember one thing: climbers place little value in the majority of climbing walls because they were designed by architects as sculptures rather than by climbers with the real thing in mind. The problems they offer are not real rock face ones. However, certain climbing walls – as at Leeds University, Rothwell Sports Centre and the Sobell Centre in North London – are first-class.

For the moment, though, let us stick to the climbing immediately on the doorstep: the boulder problems right at home on which you can begin learning now.

HOW TO GARDEN A ROCK FACE

Climbers pioneering a previously unexplored route go to some lengths to strip the rock of vegetation growing on ledges, in cracks – in fact wherever it covers holds. This procedure is known as 'gardening' and you should garden your immediate climbing problems now because the edge of a training shoe sole is not going to stay on a tiny foothold covered with moss or soil. It is amazing how a vegetated surface can seem to give no climbing chance whatsoever, yet when stripped of 'veg' the possibilities of good climbing stand out as if spotlit.

Use a penknife for cleaning cracks and holds, and then go over them again with a wire brush. Finally wait for a dry day and go over everything with a bristle floor brush so that mud is never trampled into the holds.

The more you garden your boulder problems the more chances you have of finding loose holds in advance – bricks that are loose, stones that crumble, pieces of rock which split away. Clean it all away so that the surface remaining is firm and solid. You can always test for loose holds by banging a suspected hold first with the heel of a hand. Listen when compared with a solid handhold – a rotten grip will sound cracked. And a warning: if climbing on rocks in a park or on an embankment where it is obvious others have been before (signs: lots of shoe-polished footholds and grafiti scratched all over) check ledges first for broken bottles as these are just the place to find sharp bits of glass.

Lastly, check the ground beneath. Remove any large stones and the loose bricks or rocks you may have dropped during the gardening operations. Anything which might possibly injure you if you fell awkwardly needs to be taken well away. And traplike holes and hollows which could also turn an ankle or twist you off-balance need filling with soil, gravel, sand, leaves or any other soft debris. Look for snags like broken glass too on the ground.

It is easy to fall into the temptation of leaning bricks or large stones up against the 'boulder' when you wish to try a move or two higher on the boulder but find it impossible to leave the ground because there are no holds. Remove such cheating aids from the start. They are unnecessary and present an awkward landing if you drop from those higher moves above.

CLIMBING BOULDERS ON YOUR DOORSTEP

It is no coincidence that some of the greatest climbers like Reinhold Messner (he has climbed many tremendous Alpine faces solo) spend hours bouldering; Messner, in fact, tells in his book, *The Seventh Grade*, of daily traversing along a beading on the wall of the students quarters, once each way, making nearly 60 metres in all to develop his forearm muscles, and also of traversing at an old saw-mill – this traverse being 80 metres long and the holds, on average, no more than three metres above the ground – until his fingers got cramp and he had to let go and fall off. You can do the same.

Make a saw-mill traverse

The saw-mill traverse can be copied on any boulder problem you discover locally. Not only will it give you proficiency if you stick at it, but such a traverse will help develop stronger fingers too. Simply climb the first two or three feet off the ground after checking the approximate 'line' of the traverse along the footholds and handholds you can see, then step out along it – placing the edge of each foot just beneath the big toe on hold after hold. You will soon get the idea of tentatively re-positioning each foot until it feels settled and before committing your weight to it on small edges of brick or stone. Now you are really climbing – the pawing, testing, thinking and moving are all involved in every move you make, and it's something to be learned slowly.

This experiment, simple as it may seem, will certainly hammer home some basic truths because you are actually climbing, no matter how near the ground, and not just reading about it. For example: how to drop the heel so that you press with the toes in just the right position and extra hard; how to keep your hands low rather than reaching high and becoming trapped, unable to go up or down a steep face be it a house wall or tree trunk; and how leg muscles and good footwork are more important at first than biceps and arm strength. We will deal with all these points in this chapter and there are many. Even striding from one foothold to another some distance away can seem a formidable task inches above the ground when you want to avoid the ground at all costs. So let's go to it now.

First, then, the footholds you will use.

DISCOVERING FOOTHOLDS

Learn to look first for footholds, *then* for handholds. If you make this a habit from the start you set off on the right footing as using footholds correctly is vital when you are still a beginner. There are three basic kinds.

Incuts

Incut footholds vary in size from flat ledges on which you can place a good amount of your foot to the smallest nicks which will house the merest edge of your boot – or, to see it even better, a ½p coin and not laid flat at that but on its side! Insignificant as such a tiny hold may seem that's all you may have to help you on some moves – the slightest ripple, flaw or crystal on which, so long as it is 'incut', you can position the edge of your foot and move upwards or across from the 'launching pad', as it were, that it provides.

Bevelled holds

Rounded, as opposed to incut, holds can bulge outwards or slope inwards – convex or concave. Either way they do not seem to offer anywhere near the same support as good incuts until you have gained the knack of flexing the ankle and turning the toes inwards – a technique known as 'smearing' where you scrunch the rubber sole (especially a flexible sole like a gymn shoe) into the rock so you feel any roughnesses biting into the rubber. Many holds on popular routes were once of the 'incut' variety but are now rounded by constant use and you really need to persevere before you can stand comfortably on such slippery-looking supports.

Smooth footholds

Flat surfaces of bricks, stone or rock can all be used by the feet because you press the sole against them in passing to help shove you en route for a small incut or bevelled nub which constitutes a rather better but still brief resting place while still en route for the bigger incut which make the best resting place, and from which you survey the next sequence of moves ahead. That's the way climbers think – and move . . . But although such smooth footholds may have a basic roughness which help give passing purchase to the feet you need something else, too – unless the angle is so gentle that you can pad up perfectly smooth rock on the friction of your boot soles alone. And that 'something' is handholds which, in combination, help to force the foot on to the smooth face and keep it there.

FINDING HANDHOLDS

There are more kinds of handholds than footholds. For one thing almost any hold that can be used by the feet can be used by the hands; for another, holds that are useless for the feet can still be used by the hands as fingers are able to grip in more variety of ways and arms can't only pull but push too.

Jugs

'Jughandles' are monster holds which allow the hands or fingers (yes, there are even 'fingerjugs') to curl right over as they would a rail in the swimming pool when you wish to haul yourself out.

Incuts

Incuts, already discussed, are much more common than jugs. A climbing move may call for just one fingertip pressing on an incut to keep the body in balance as you step higher. And, tiny as it seems, it is adequate. Sometimes incuts are larger, however, and you can find a shelf like a window sill which offers a flat-topped hold for both hands. This not only gives you something to pull up on, but also a good resting place to stand on.

Undercuts

'Upside down' holds are used by feeling with the fingers from beneath, then pulling outwards – as you would if you opened a matchbox and all the matches fell out. They are invaluable when there is nothing else to keep you in balance – for by grasping an undercut with one hand you can reach higher with the other hand. Or you can actually move the feet up while holding the undercut with both hands and then, when the feet are on holds, reach one-handed for a high hold.

Sideholds

Another way of keeping in balance is by reaching out for a sidehold – say the edge of a window or the corner of a building – and pulling towards you. So long as the footholds are suitably placed so that you can stand in balance, your other hand can roam above in search for other handholds.

Pinch grips

If a fingerful of rock can be squeezed, nipped or pinched between the fingers and thumb it could be useful for maintaining your balance when the rock is otherwise smooth.

Pressure holds

Hands can be used on your bevelled and smooth-type footholds, too – not, of course, by pulling on them ladder-rung fashion which is impossible as there is no purchase for the fingers to cling with, but by pressing down or sideways against them with the heel of the hand or the fingertips. There are many permutations of these moves ranging from climbing a rock slab for several feet by pressing down with both hands – as well as feet – to the mantelshelf where both hands reach up above your head to a window sill, say, then you pull up on the arms, press down with the hands and so monkey on up to the shelf.

Pressure holds are especially important because they happen all the time and their use to the beginner is never obvious at first. This is because the newcomer thinks only in terms of handholds as being of the clinging-type or ladder rung jughandle variety. Nothing is further from the truth; and you should learn to look on such good holds as the luxuries they are – only occasionally to be relished even on easy climbs. It is pressure holds, in fact, which are so often the clue to solving 'impossible' climbing problems. Here is an example.

Take a strong wooden table that comes to about or above waist height and place it against the trunk of a tree or a wall where there are handholds above – a branch or ledge – and just within reach. Grasp the branch or ledge with both hands and try to step up on to the table top without using a knee. Most people will find it impossible because the table is too high. Yet a pressure hold will solve your problem in a moment. Simply pull on the branch or ledge with one hand and press down on the table top with the other. You can now swing a foot up easily like the best of them, then straighten up and stand on your 'ledge'. Always watch for similar movements which can make your climbing much less of a struggle.

TRAVERSING VARIATIONS

Try the following traversing problems once you have worked out simple traverses near home.

Miss-the-hold

Ban the use of certain footholds or handholds which otherwise make a traverse you have already accomplished too easy. Anyone who has to use them or falls off must start again.

Handicap traverse

Carry a rucksack or converted duffel bag (see Ch. 3) on your back – full of books or stones. The extra weight will mean you must pay extra attention to footholds and balance.

Climb one-handed

Stick a hand in your pocket and try to cross a traverse by using only the other. Although this seems impossible at first you will be surprised how by compensating for the lack of a hand with extra careful footwork you can still manage.

Climb no-hands

When the angle of an embankment allows, and it can still be quite steep, place both hands in the pockets and make your way across on the feet alone – although here you are also allowed to use forehead, elbow and knee as props when needed. Gradually, however, you can even eliminate these.

Footswapping traverse

Cross your traverse in a series of foot-changing moves on all the holds. Stride left, for instance, on to the first hold of the traverse, stop and then change feet on it. Step left again and again change feet – and so on.

Crossed leg traversing

Instead of changing feet on each hold, try traversing by putting a foot 'through' each time – as described earlier in this chapter.

Hand traversing

Try this manoeuvre: choose a strong tree branch low enough to be just out of reach at full arms stretch about ten feet from the tree trunk. Jump up and grasp with both hands. Now move hand after hand (NOT hand over hand which leads to crossed hands and wrists and which make for bad climbing) until you can touch the trunk and climb down the inch or two to the ground. Occasionally you will have to make a hand traverse high on a rock face and this is good training.

Chain traversing

Climb back and forth across a traverse without stopping to touch the ground until your fingers fail and you have to jump down. See who can do the most traversing without touching the ground.

Cross-country traversing

Any stretch of park, common, fields, downs, coastline, moor or woods is fair game for a long distance traverse. You pick a starting point and, several hundred yards away, a finish. The contest is to find who can reach the finishing point without touching grass. The moment you do touch so much as a blade of grass – deduct 10 points. The winner is the one to finish with least number of points.

Although you are not allowed to touch the ground, it doesn't mean you cannot use stream beds, tree trunks, low branches, strong fence posts, solid walls, isolated boulders and tree stumps, fallen logs, old railings and so on. Many of the movements from one refuge to the next may be quite acrobatic, but set a height limit of ten feet to avoid high-level traversing along buildings or tree boughs. And do make sure all walls and fence posts along your route are really strong and cannot be weakened or moved by your efforts first.

DIRECT ASCENTS

The following experiments should be tried on boulders that are no higher than twice your own height with arms raised upwards at full stretch. If this still doesn't seem very high you will be surprised just how far away the ground does appear when you are nearing the top of such a little Everest and you need to pluck up all the nerve you can find to finish. In case you fall, of course, you have prepared the ground below first.

MAKE SAFE LANDINGS

A really soft landing can be made from old mattresses, banks of sand or gravel, heaps of hay, bracken and autumn leaves or even by binding strong cardboard boxes tightly together with string – a favourite of film stunt men who might have to cushion an eighty-foot fall. Snowdrifts too are excellent shock-absorbers if you are fortunate enough to have boulder problems directly above them. Whatever you do use – the ground must be soft and clean. Mud, for example, may seem good enough, but once you start to climb again you smear the holds with grease.

When satisfied that your landings are safe try the following experiments.

STAKE A SMALL BET ON A BOULDER PROBLEM

The chief requirement, besides a good landing, is a slab climb – a brick, stone or rock face lying back at an angle of around 60°–75°. It could be a seaside or old railway embankment – anything like that. The point being, however, that your route up this miniature face should be so smooth and difficult that you only manage to climb it after many attempts and that – this is most important – the very last move when you are about twice your own height from the ground should involve a very long stretch for the top where, in fact, the finishing holds are just slightly out of reach from the last reasonable footholds beneath. Which means, in fact, that to make the top you need to climb up two or three more moves on much smaller footholds rather than in one tempting lunge. This is the whole point of it all . . .

When you have taped this problem so that you can repeat it again and again, challenge your friends – by placing a small coin on the finishing handhold. Whoever can reach it first without falling off keeps the coin. And draw from a fistful of grasses as to who goes first – longest grass goes last. You can almost be sure, however, that if you have worked out this climbing problem correctly your money is safe.

Climber after climber will slide back down the slab only just failing to reach the coin each time. This is because the sight of the prize apparently at last within reach makes them break a basic climbing principle: never lift the heels. Instead of padding up the final few feet in carefully thought-out moves they make a long lurch at full stretch and grab. Imagine it – this raises the heels and as feet lift, the toes slip and your feet shoot off.

Always remember, therefore, to cut out that greedy feeling in snatching for what may (or may not) be big holds, and concentrate instead on making the most of the available holds directly in front of you which will usually be small. In this case, of course, reaching for the coin was the aim, but on a real rock climb a large handhold above is the same sort of prize when you are in need of its security after a tricky stretch of climbing.

Hand in hand with keeping the heels low are other key principles you also learn here: keep your head down and watch the feet before reaching for handholds . . . choose small footholds close together rather than larger footholds much further apart . . . learn to balance on the feet rather than pulling with the hands to ensure that you are rarely pressed against the face (yes, there should be plenty of daylight showing between you and the face) . . . and by working out each move from small hold to small hold beforehand – instead of lurching and grabbing anything that comes to hand – much better climbing progress is made.

This is fine, of course, when there are holds. But what about when you face a completely bald surface?

HOW TO CLIMB SHEER WALLS

The smoothest side of a house can be climbed if you use pressure in much the same way as you can push a car that has stalled by putting your back against it and pressing hard with the legs. To be able to do this on a sheer rock face must mean, however, that there is another face either opposite or adjacent to it to give you the purchase needed. Just how the two walls are positioned determines the type of technique you use. These methods are the basis of all serious climbing problems when actual holds are scarce and there are many stretches of smooth rock to be overcome.

Chimneying

The most obvious way of using pressure where you literally push your way upwards is to brace yourself between two corridor or passage walls about three feet apart as already mentioned, and where dirty footprints are tolerated. To be safe: climb no higher than to twice your height, remember. Such a cleft is equivalent to a rock face chimney which can split a crag for hundreds of feet.

Backing and footing is the key to cracking it. Push your back against one side and, one after the other, your feet well up against the far wall. In fact, you can practise it now across almost any open doorway. This resting position now gained is so safe you can catch a tennis ball thrown to you down the alley without effort. And how to move?

Take one foot from the wall in front and place it below you and against the wall behind. Press downwards, too, with both hands by the hips. And push yourself away from the rear wall with that back foot, keep forcing with the front foot and then re-rest your back higher up on the rear wall. Transfer the foot below and behind you back on the wall in front at a high enough level for you to feel comfortable. And then repeat the moving-up sequence either with the same foot behind which you used before or with the other foot – and so on. You can rest whenever you wish by pressing both feet out in front and taking a breather.

When the walls are close together your style will become more cramped – you may even have to use the knees. You will also really have to stretch across when the walls are at your limit of reaching with the legs. The thing to do is – practise on as many passages and corridors and doorways as you can find and you will discover how different widths affect your technique.

And how do you climb back down? Simply reverse the procedure of placing the feet, keep pushing, and lower yourself down like a lift on the hydraulic buffers of your legs which are locked in place across the gap. Instead of pushing your way up

Chimneying

you push yourself down; it is as easy to descend as it was to go up on a chimney of more or less the right width.

Bridging

When chimney walls are so far apart you can't quite reach the far side with your feet and yet where there are footholds on both sides another method is called for – 'bridging'. This means you face up or down the passage or corridor rather than across it and climb it with a foot and a hand on each side – and using whichever footholds and handholds become available. This is not an easy technique, and the beginner will need actual holds on both walls for support. The more you do practise, however, the easier it becomes and you will be able to graduate to the time when you can still 'bridge' up even when there are no holds in view at all because you rely on sheer pressure to do the work: that means your feet stay stuck against the wall, locked in place by pressure alone from your leg muscles – and your hands also stick flat on the wall, fingers pointing down and the heels of the hands pushing against the chimney sides, as you force downwards with the arms. As strenuous as this technique is, especially while pushing and levering yourself up-

Bridging

wards as a result, it is nevertheless helped by the appearance of occasional holds.

Such holds are ideal resting places where you can re-assess your position as you straddle the 'void'. For example, the chimney walls may have been growing closer all the time without your realising it. Now, at rest, you see how you need no longer bridge up the chimney, but can transfer into a more comfortable back-and-foot position instead. The ways you change your posture and positions in climbing are legion, and nowhere is this more necessary than when bridging.

Even chimneys are not necessary for bridging technique, however. There are two other rock face features which you might climb for much of the way bridged out across the drop and forcing your way on up rock which, to a novice, seems to offer no chance of holds of any kind; they are 'grooves' and 'corners'. And you can find a fair copy of their problems wherever playground, gymnasium or garage walls meet in a corner which you can try and climb – using the brickwork as holds.

Any channel which cuts the rock like a half-opened book, and which lies back at a steep angle is a 'groove'. The walls are sometimes smooth – and you cannot usually back-and-foot up grooves because of the angle of these walls. The answer is to bridge across, foot and hand on each wall, and sometimes finding holds in the very back of the groove where the walls join too. By pressing down with one or both hands on wrinkles and flanges and small dimples in the rock . . . and by forcing the feet sideways on such minute holds, too, the good climber can work a spectacular way up really formidable-looking rock as he straddles across thin air.

As for 'corners' – these are really vertical grooves with their walls more or less set at 90° to each other. Their steepness make them strenuous and they call for a combination of bridging and chimneying with – let's not forget – excursions into the very angle of the corner where holds can sometimes be found, too. The key hold here is often the vertical crack which acts as a kind of guttering or open drainpipe down the back. Such a hold is a speciality in itself and you can learn how to use vertical cracks a little later in the chapter. First, however, let's look at the final kind of move which can breach a sheer wall.

Mantelshelfing

Mantelshelfing has been mentioned previously as a way of using pressure holds when the sheer wall is only really smooth for the few feet directly in front of you. And above the holdless stretch is a small ledge or shelf which you can grasp with both hands. The ideal example close to home is a window ledge which you can just about reach standing on tiptoe and with both arms fully stretched overhead.

Reach for the 'mantelshelf', grasp it two-handed and pull yourself up on the arms. You can help your movements by running the feet up the side of the building as you go. Now comes the application of downwards pressure . . . As your chest comes level with the shelf, throw an elbow on to it, then the other – both forearms now lying on top and fingers touching. Flip one elbow high and straighten the arm while pressing hard downwards, then do the same with the other. Doing this jacks your body up even further, and you can run your toes up the face to help even more. As your belt buckle levels with the ledge keep pressing with the arms and throw a knee or preferably a foot up on to the shelf and stand up – your hands keeping you in balance from holds which become available as you straighten up on the power of your leg muscles. Mantelshelf moves can prove easier than this sounds too where tiny footholds on the face allow you to climb quite high without the strain on the arms caused by chinning up all the way.

HOW TO CLIMB VERTICAL CRACKS

Just as chimneys offer a feasible way of breaching holdless rock, so vertical cracks several inches wide serve the same purpose. Not that you can climb inside them – they are too narrow. Instead, the climber has to use hands, feet and – where the crack is wide enough – an arm and leg inside the fissure. The following experiments will show you what I mean.

Climb a wedging crack

Any vertical slit, possibly between two adjacent buildings, which will just allow an arm and a leg inside will give you the idea of how to climb a rock face crack of similar width. This kind of climbing can be a struggle even for a good climber – so be warned! The snag is that so often footholds inside the cleft are rare – usually non-existent, in fact – and that you are constantly fighting against the tendency to slip back down after making a foot or two of hard won height. There are ways to lock yourself in position, however, and it is these you must use in helping to propel you upwards too.

Firstly, brace your shoulder, elbow and a heel of a hand inside the crack: by pressing with all three points on both opposite walls you can win a good leverage which will – when done properly – enable you to climb arm over arm up the crack. You lock each arm in place as you go, only relaxing one arm when the one above it is securely jammed in place. You then take the lower arm out of the crack and replace it once more above the well-wedged arm – and so on. But what about the feet? They too can be wedged one above the other by: a) bending the knee to one side so you can insert the foot or toes into the crack *sideways*, and b) straightening your foot in the crack, then c) putting your weight on it. (To free the foot – do the opposite.) You must be ready to practise hard because such 'thrutching' cracks as they are called – 'thrutching' means fighting – can be unpleasant and at first seem quite impossible to the beginner. Sometimes, of course a crack suitable for wedging is too wide for the feet used this way and instead you should face sideways on to the rock and after bracing yourself with an arm inside as described, insert a foot across the crack with the toe pressed sideways against one side and the heel against the other. You push downwards with the other hand on the edge of the crack pressure hold-style, or else reach for possible holds above and – still facing sideways on – ascend by repeatedly levering your way up, locking yourself in position, then pushing your way up again and so on. Lastly: two points. Avoid trying to squeeze your body into such tight places – you could become stuck if you are small enough to squirm part-way inside. And watch out for footholds on the very edge of such a crack which, of course, make the climbing much easier and which make trying to thrutch your way up a pointless exercise if you were ascending a real rock climb.

Learn to layback

There is a type of vertical crack which runs up the junction where the walls of a corner or groove meet and which allows you to climb completely bald rock. The technique is called a 'layback' and it is strenuous because that is exactly what you do: you 'layback' on your arms and press your feet high on to the face in front of you like a monkey on a stick.

Look for a layback crack where two brick or stone walls join – old buildings and embankments often have them. And even if there isn't much of a vertical crack to be seen in the corner, you can sometimes use the edges of protruding bricks or chunks of stone as handholds for laybacking.

To start: standing facing into the corner and run both hands up inside the crack which should have a good sharp edge so that your fingers can curl around it; now pull backwards on the arms, lift one foot high and press it against the wall facing you AND . . . place the other foot next to it. If you are pulling hard enough, the feet will stick in place even on a smooth vertical surface. Run the hands up the crack together, first one then the other, and shuffle the feet upwards too to keep pace and to keep them high. Don't hang about once you do start – it is a tiring technique.

And a tip to start with: if there are actual footholds on your practise layback use them at first as lean back on the arms. But once you find the footholds make the climbing too easy – and you will – avoid placing the foot on them and, instead, pad only up the smooth parts of the facing wall.

Climb a tree with boxing gloves
No, although there is a joke about climbing in boxing gloves and roller skates which means a climb must be very easy indeed, this is a serious experiment. The purpose of it is to show how to jam your hands in vertical rock face cracks the way the experts do when a rock face is otherwise devoid of handholds and footholds. Of course, the hard men don't carry an old pair of boxing gloves as I suggest you use here – they swarm up on their bare fists alone. But boxing gloves will help make it more comfortable for you as well as easier to get a purchase at this early stage. It is not an easy technique even so, but it is a method which is necessary if you plan to take up climbing seriously. And you can try it now on trees.

Look for trees where two or three trunks grow from one

bole. The gap between each trunk should be so narrow that they do in fact present vertical rock face-type 'cracks', narrowing at the bottom where they join. There are also good 'cracks' formed in the 'V' where branches grow from a trunk at a narrow angle and also where branches themselves fork narrowly into further branches. All of these 'crack'-type handholds can be used in practise in two ways.

One is that you actually climb up the tree for several feet excluding the use of any other handhold except jamming your hands in the 'cracks' between the trunks and branches . . . and then you climb back down again. For instance, you could begin by jamming your left fist between two trunks growing close together from the bole of the same tree, and pulling up on the arm so your feet can reach high footholds on the bark. The trunks are still close enough to allow you to jam the other hand higher still, between the trunks but then the gap opens out and now you need some other jamming hold for the left hand. But a bough growing out overhead forks into two separate branches and you can reach up with your left fist and jam it into the 'V'.

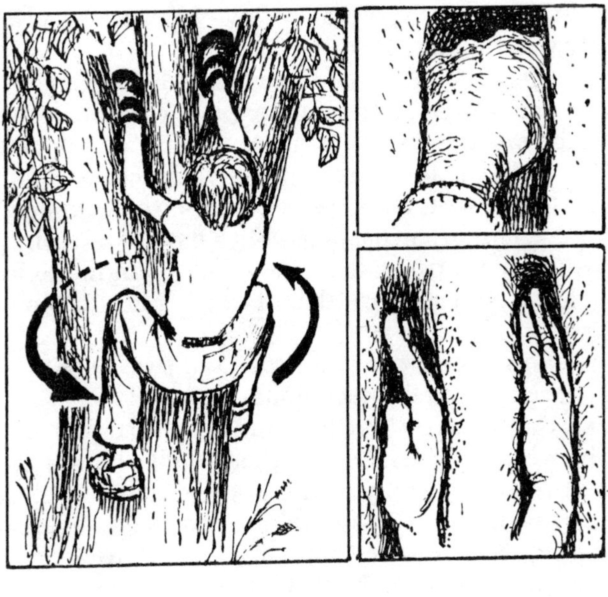

You move up once more, and higher still is another 'V' between branches for your right fist. And now you climb back down using the same holds but in reverse. Well, that is one way of learning to hand jam. The other method is to make a girdle traverse around a huge trunk about four feet from the ground and using only hand jams as holds in whatever rock-type 'cracks' are available. Of course, you must first find a tree which has such natural 'cracks' – there are plenty of them about.

As to the actual technique of hand jamming, the first thing is not to be afraid of hurting your hands. This is why old boxing gloves will break you into the idea of supporting your weight from jammed hands gently. You also find how really effective such handholds are – especially when you are growing tired and still your hands lock you in position (unlike an orthodox ladder rung-type handhold where exhausted fingers open out and you fall). However, there comes a time when to progress you must take the gloves off. (Incidentally, a safety point: to avoid ever being caught should your gloves accidentally jam fast so well you can't free them always (a) avoid lacing them up in the first place (b) have pals below who can steady your feet while you tug the gloves free.)

It is now that you make a discovery: while hanging on with the fists is one way of hand jamming, it is only one of many. And, in fact, most times you jam by inserting a limp hand flat into a crack that is too narrow for a clenched fist and then make that hand swell. Hand jams are far more common, and often more reliable, than fist jams which have to be really good to be effective. Poor fist jams are very dodgy handholds indeed because they feel so good yet the fist can fly out without warning.

The most basic kind of hand jam – and even here there are different variations to this technique – is as follows . . . Find a narrow crack on a tree where two trunks are so closely aligned the gap between is only wide enough to admit a hand slotted in flat. Insert the hand gently at full arms stretch and place the thumb across the palm. Now feel around in the 'crack' until you find just that right spot where the hand will stick firm. You will do best here to move the hand up into the wider part just above where the two trunks narrow and join. You then draw the hand carefully down into – and if possible, behind – this bottleneck until it feels nice and solid enough for you to pull up on it. With a good 'crack' it's easy, but the same advice goes here as my earlier advice about not expecting jughandles every time you reach for a handhold. There will be many occasions when your vertical crack offers only poor hand jams, and now is the time to experiment with your bare hands in all kinds of tree 'cracks' so that you learn to jam adequately even in an inadequate slot. You should never anticipate good jams – just be agreeably surprised when occasionally you find them.

Variations on the basic hand jam as just described are: crossing the fingers in a crack of just the right width . . . inserting a hand upside down and pressing back on the lip of the crevice with the thumb splayed backwards to give an opposing pressure (the upside down hand jam is particularly effective in any shape or form as it causes a twisting action of the wrist which locks the fingers even more solidly in position) . . . drawing the hand down into a crack 'bottleneck' which is narrow enough to lock the hand on its own without your needing to place the thumb across the palm . . . inserting the hand upside down this time with the thumb tucked into the back of the crack . . . and so on. The positions and possibilities are many and depend on the shape and width of the crack in each case. Try them for yourself on as many different sizes of tree 'crack' as you can find.

REVERSING

Make a point of climbing back down the boulder problems you ascend from the beginning. You never know when you may need to reverse certain moves on a rock climb, and climbing down will also help your technique because you gain a new perspective. In my book, *Survival for Young People*, I describe a way of jumping safely from a first floor window of a burning building by letting yourself hang from your hands which grasp the window ledge. If you did not realise this simple method of lessening the height to fall, you might stand on the window ledge instead just prior to leaping from it and possible freeze there with fright – it looks much further to drop than when you hang from the hands. Well, this is exactly the same mental block which must be overcome in climbing down a rock face.

A glance below at the moves to be descended, and it seems much further than it actually is. Also, as you are looking at the ground in one fell swoop you immediately start thinking about falling in one fell swoop too, because you can no longer see the holds below. As these holds will only appear when you begin climbing towards them, you must start by thinking on the same lines as letting yourself hang from that first floor window ledge of a burning building. And actually begin moving back down the face in the hope that holds will appear. If you have already climbed up this way, they will, don't worry!

The mechanics of descent are simple. Aim for the good climbing style already described where footwork is the key. Face out coming down easy-angled faces and choose your handholds as low down as possible. Lower your body down, use the footholds as they come, and then select low handholds again. If you find you have lowered yourself and can't quite reach the footholds below, you are not doing it right – go back up and choose lower handholds still. And remember that footholds are never as far beneath you as they look.

Turn sideways as the face becomes steeper. And actually face in to the boulder problem when it is steep or vertical. Choosing low handholds becomes really important now and you must become accustomed to reaching down to about waist level or below for your handholds, lowering your body down past them, and then repeating this business again. Once most of your body weight is below the handholds you will find descent much simpler than it looks. And you can hang out from the face on your fingers and really examine the footholds below whenever good handholds are at hand. Incidentally, never be afraid of lowering yourself down to full arm's stretch from decent handholds only to find no footholds below and then discover you have no strength left to pull yourself back up. Lowering your body in this way takes a lot less effort than you might imagine, and if it does become a case of finding nothing for the feet below after all, you will find you can climb back up again to your original position without too much trouble. And next time, have even lower handholds in your clutches!

Bouldering gives you that first inkling, when done seriously, of the demands of climbing – when, for instance, after a hard bouldering session you have to sip your lemonade shandy with a straw (your fingers are too tired to hold the glass!) However, bouldering is not an end in itself. If you never try out the skills you learn near ground-level, on mountains you are like a youth who learns to trap a football perfectly yet never plays a real game.

5 Learning the Ropes

Few things give the beginner a boost like carrying the climbing rope over a shoulder. It is, after all, the badge of the climber as opposed to the walker or rambler. Modern ropes look good, too, and as they represent no small piece of investment the pride of possession is obvious. Yet the time has not yet come to buy a rope, but rather to learn how to use it in advance of that red letter day when at last you have a rope of your own.

Handling the rope can call for more sweat and tears from the beginner than the actual business of where to press the feet, place the hands and look for holds. It seems so complex when it comes to the point of manipulating the leader's rope and you realise his safety hangs on your deftness and care with the nylon line. Even though your companion climber only moves up at snail's pace, it can still prove next to impossible to keep pace with paying out the rope when you are all fingers and thumbs. Then you are conscious of the exposed drop down past your ledge – and this makes things worse. If the ropes inexorably become entangled into a ball of knitting when the leader is working out a crucial move – danger! There is a good chance the beginner will panic and actually pull the leading climber off his holds in a desperate effort to get the ropes sorted out.

Yet basically rope technique is simple. You can practise the handful of necessary knots at home with a shoelace or bit of string, and learn the nuts and bolts of roped climbing sequence with a hank of plastic clothes line. And this includes simulating falls – and fielding a tumbling partner on the rope too. Thus when your time comes to grapple with your first rock face, the rope work comes so comfortably you can give the actual climbing the attention it deserves instead of getting tied up in knots at every opportunity.

FUN WITH BASIC KNOTS

The first thing you must know about handling climbing ropes is how to tie them. Practise at home first, and the following experiments will ensure that not only do you tie the knots correctly – a vital business in climbing – but that you will remember them more easily when it is necessary to use such and such a knot immediately.

Buy a hank of plastic clothes line from a hardware store. It should be synthetic because then it will be more representative of a perlon or nylon climbing rope though, of course, only a fraction as strong. Knots tied in such climbing ropes tend to creep as they will in a synthetic clothes line – so you learn how to allow for this failing from the beginning. You need 15 metres (about 48ft) and it will cost less than 50p. Buy a bright colour, and seal the ends in a match flame to make solid tips which won't unravel.

You will also need a karabiner. Buy one with a screw gate from a climbing shop – see Chapter 2 on *Equipment*. (If you don't take to climbing after all, the krab will still be useful as bicycle lock; have a hole drilled in the karabiner where the sleeve is locking the gate in position, slip a small lock through the hole after clipping the krab across the front wheel spokes and turn the key.)

Lastly, you need a couple of nylon shoelaces, a piece of cord about the same length and also a similar length of stiffish canvas tape bought off the haberdashery counter at Woolworths.

ON NO ACCOUNT MUST YOU USE CLOTHES LINE FOR CLIMBING. THIS WARNING CANNOT BE STRESSED ENOUGH. THE ONLY POSSIBLE USE FOR SUCH A FRAIL AND UTTERLY UNDEPENDABLE 'ROPE' IS AS A MEANS OF PRACTISING KNOTS AND ROPE HANDLING BEFORE YOU EVER SET FOOT ON ROCK– WHERE ONLY A PROPER CLIMBING ROPE WILL SUFFICE.

And now for the knots which will always stand you in good stead throughout your climbing career.

THE FIGURE OF EIGHT KNOT

The figure of eight knot is the most basic knot in climbing. Not only is it by far the easiest to tie, but you can tie it wrongly and it will still hold a falling climber. Other good things about this knot are that it is stronger than a bowline – the classic climbing knot for tying yourself to the rope – and that it can be used in so many ways. Not only can you tie yourself to the rope but it can be used for looping over rock face spikes and flakes when belaying, as we will see presently. You can, in fact, climb a rock face roped to another climber from bottom to top and only *one* knot is used throughout the climb for every operation – this very simple and versatile figure of eight fastening.

Tie a figure of eight knot around your waist

Tie it now and adjust it round your waist – by feeding one strand of the rope through the knot and tightening it afterwards as shown (you may seem all thumbs at first but it soon becomes easy). Because your synthetic clothes line is rather 'greasy' and knots tend to slacken after a little while – as they do in man-made climbing rope, too – tie the end tail off with a thumb knot around the main rope as shown to check any unloosening tendencies.

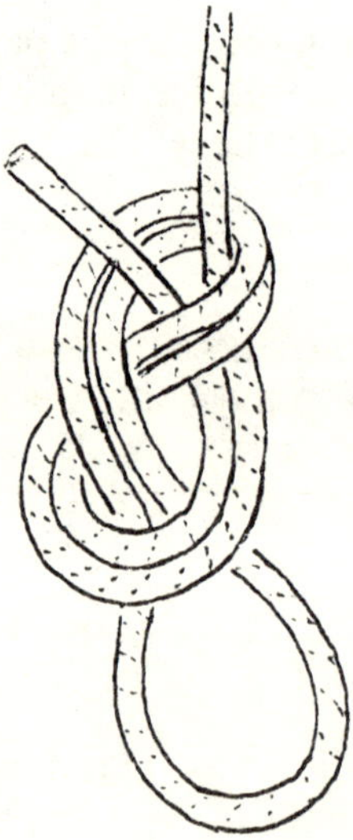

Make a mess of a figure of eight knot – and still be safe

The easiest way to make an error with this knot is to tie an ordinary overhand knot instead of a figure of eight. Do this now. Tie two nylon shoelaces, or each end of your plastic line, in two separate loops – one with an overhand, the other with a figure of eight – over a fence post or door knob. Now pull really hard on both lengths of lace or line leading to the loops. And examine the knots. The one which was tied incorrectly – the overhand knot – still held didn't it? It didn't slip either, did it? However it is when you come to untie them that you realise how much easier the figure of eight knot is to untie – a real advantage on the rock face.

Try a figure of eight harness tie-on

As mentioned in Chapter 2, belts and harnesses are now worn around the body by the majority of climbers. They are more convenient and safer than the rope alone tied around the waist – although the rope waistline is quite satisfactory for introductory rock climbs. Most climbing schools today, however, prefer students to wear climbing belts. Tying into them is simple. Imagine the ordinary leather belt around your waist is a climbing belt – it isn't, of course, and must never be used as one, but you can still imagine. Clip the karabiner to it. Tie a small figure of eight knot into the end of your plastic line. Finish it off with a thumb knot, and clip this into the karabiner. Screw up the sleeve on the gate to secure it and you are attached to the 'rope' correctly. (Many climbing belts have a sliding shackle – the karabiner would be clipped into this rather than round the belt as you did on this occasion, but it's the same principle.)

Tie a figure of eight one-handed

Race a friend: see who can tie the knot first with one hand in a pocket. Simply tie both ends of a shoelace or piece of string to a table leg. Now work out the way to pull the doubled shoelace taut between all the fingers and a thumb of one hand an inch or two from the end and wrap the tip of the loop twice round the two lengths of shoelace or string with a finger and thumb before – tricky this – pulling the tip of the loop back through itself. Then pull tight.

THE BOWLINE

The bowline has always been the traditional way of tying the end of the rope around your waist, and many climbers still use it. Although weaker than the figure of eight nor as simple, it is easier to adjust once around your body if you learned this knot before the figure of eight. It is also used as a tie-in for climbing belts.

Knot a bowline around your waist

The diagram shows how. Adjust by feeding the rope through one side of the knot until the waist loop feels snug and tight. And tie two half-hitches on the end tail.

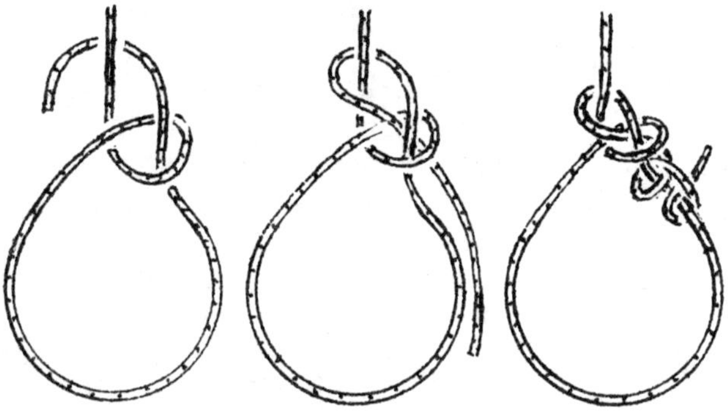

Tie an idiot-proof bowline

Try wiring a 'tucked' bowline which will check any possibility of the knot working loose. (Still check it often, all the same!). Incidentally this 'tucked' finish can also complete a figure of eight knot.

Tie a bowline that won't jam

An even better variation of the bowline can be made simply by doubling up on the very first loop – as shown. Tie one end of your plastic line in a normal bowline, and the other end in a double-knotted bowline. Drop both loops over a fence post and pull on them hard, lasso-fashion. Undo the knots and you will see just how much more easily the double-knotted bowline is untied. Make it a habit always to tie the double-knotted bowline instead of the ordinary knot when you use a bowline waistline. (This knot stays more firmly knotted during use as well; the ordinary bowline tends to slacken off a little.) And 'tuck' the end in as above.

THE FISHERMAN'S KNOT

Here is a knot for joining two climbing ropes, or the ends of a length of rope to make a loop. It is the only knot for nylon or perlon rope, as it won't slip. To prove it . . .

The only knot to hitch your trousers up with slippery rope
Slip on a pair of trousers which allow for a belt to stop them from slipping down. Cut off a length of plastic line several inches longer than the distance round your waist and seal both ends in a flame. Thread this through thc waist loops on your trousers. Tie it in front with a reef knot, and forget about it. You won't be able too for long, however, because this knot creeps and can actually untie itself in a short time when man-made rope is used.

Now use the double fisherman's knot as shown. The problem is solved. The knot stays put and so do your trousers. Untie the knot, remove the length of line, tie it into a loop with a double fisherman's knot and leave it to one side: this loop is an imitation 'sling' and we'll practice with it shortly.

THE TAPE KNOT

Slings can be made from nylon or perlon rope, or from nylon webbing of different widths. The only knot for webbing, how-

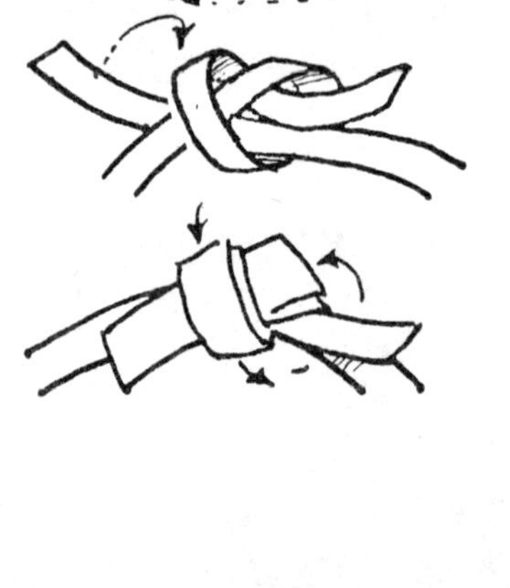

ever, is the tape knot and you can practise tying it as shown with the length of tape mentioned earlier in this chapter.

There are certain other knots which are needed occasionally on mountains. These are best dealt with as the need arises, the ones detailed so far being the basics for most climbing needs. However, you must know how to tie yourself to the face when belaying – as we saw in Chapter 1.

THE BELAY KNOTS

There are different ways of belaying yourself to a cliff depending on how you are tied to the rope, and the kinds of anchor you will be using – whether rock spike, chockstone or tree trunk. Tie the plastic line around your waist with a figure of eight knot or double knotted bowline – with 'tuck' knot to finish – and practise the following belays just as if you were actually tying yourself to the mountain and ready to safeguard your partner's rope in a field, or backyard.

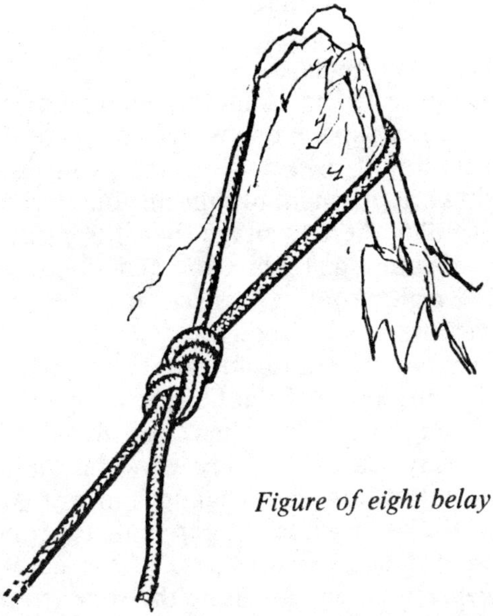

Figure of eight belay

The figure of eight belay

The simplest belay of all is to tie a figure of eight loop in the rope, drop it over a rock spike about head-level, in this case a window catch or branch stub sticking from a tree trunk, and – you are belayed. No matter if your companion falls, he cannot drag you down with him now – the loop will hold you fast.

You can learn a key principle of belaying too at this preliminary stage. It is that your belay loop should always come down tight from above to your waist – not only to hold you steady in case of a fall, but also to help keep the rope firmly in place on the belay anchor. Make sure when you tie this knot, therefore, that you can feel the belay tugging comfortably on your waist so that if someone were to push you suddenly – ask a friend to do this at *ground level*: you will survive! Gauging just the right amount of rope between the waistline and actual anchorage needs experience to get it right first time because a disadvantage of this knot as a belay is that it is not readily adjustable during the tying. First you must tie the loop in the rope, then place the loop over the spike, then settle back on the stance where it is only now you see if the belay was correctly adjusted or not in the first place.

Another spike belay knots

The diagram opposite shows another method of belaying with the rope over a rock spike: one where you place the rope over the spike, bringing it back to you, then you tie it back in a figure of eight knot in a bight of rope on your waistline.

This knot holds the advantage that it is easily adjusted to pull tightly on your waist while you actually tie it. . . . unlike the figure of eight knot. However, it is also rather more difficult to tie and needs practise.

Query: can you spot a disadvantage of this knot – when compared with the figure of eight belay? *Clue*: imagine you are belayed and your partner has fallen and is dangling on the rope far below . . . Any nearer? No? The answer is that the figure of eight belay will still allow the dangling climber to be supported directly from the belay while you can untie the rope from your waist and go for help. In the case of the other belay described, however, you cannot untie the rope from your waist

Spike belay tied back onto waistline with figure of eight knot

without also untying the belay too and so you must wait until your companion recovers enough to help himself or help arrives. It is a most extreme situation, of course, but think about it.

A thread belay knot

Supposing there are no rock spikes for anchors, but there is a good chockstone in a crack. Or a strong tree grows from the face nearby. It is impossible to loop the rope over either of these anchors lasso-fashion. Instead, take a length of the rope from the knot on your waistline, double it, pass the bight of rope round the chockstone or tree and bring it back to the waist where you tuck it back, up through the waist tie, together with an equal loop from the other rope. Tie off the two loops round all the ropes from the waist as shown here. It's easy when you try it.

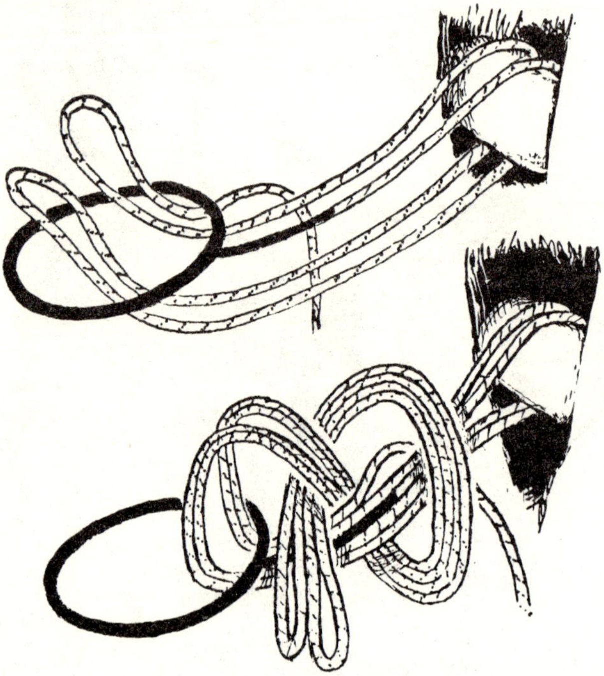

Thread belay knot

Belaying from a belt

When the rope is tied with a figure of eight knot to a screw-gate karabiner clipped to a sliding shackle on a climbing belt you need a different method. Try it now. Clip the karabiner to a leather belt around your waist and tie the plastic line to it with a figure of eight knot. Take the line over a window catch or clothes hook and tie it back on your belt with the simple spike belay knot described above. It doesn't feel right? The answer is: tie it back into the karabiner instead with a figure of eight tied into a bight of rope as shown.

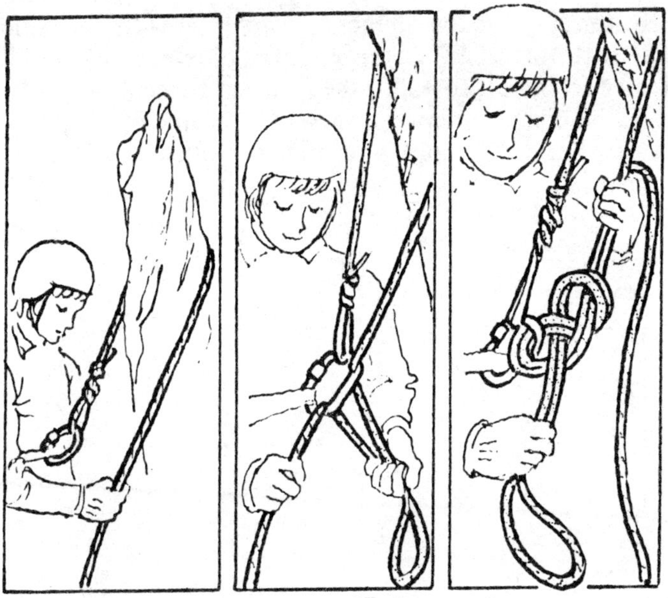

Spike belay tied back into waist belt karabiner with figure of eight knot

Query: where is the risk here? *Answer:* in untying. Beginners have been known to undo the wrong figure of eight knot in the karabiner so disconnecting themselves from the rope altogether. Be careful here.

And that's that. Enough of knots for now. The next stage is to see how to use them while actually climbing a rock face. The fact there are no crags for miles is no obstacle. You can easily simulate one where there are trees. Just imagine . . . .

CLIMB A 'ROCK FACE' IN THE PARK

Find several trees standing together in a park, wood, garden or field. Take seven or eight trees in line and several yards apart. The first tree stands for the bottom of a rock climb; the last tree in line, the summit. And each tree in between represents a stance or ledge on the way to the top with the intervals in between standing for the pitches by which all cliffs are climbed one after the other. While the length of pitches on a rock climb can vary from 15ft to 150ft, they should be kept below 50ft – that is, the distance between each of your line of trees – in the park or wherever because your plastic clothes line is less than 50ft long.

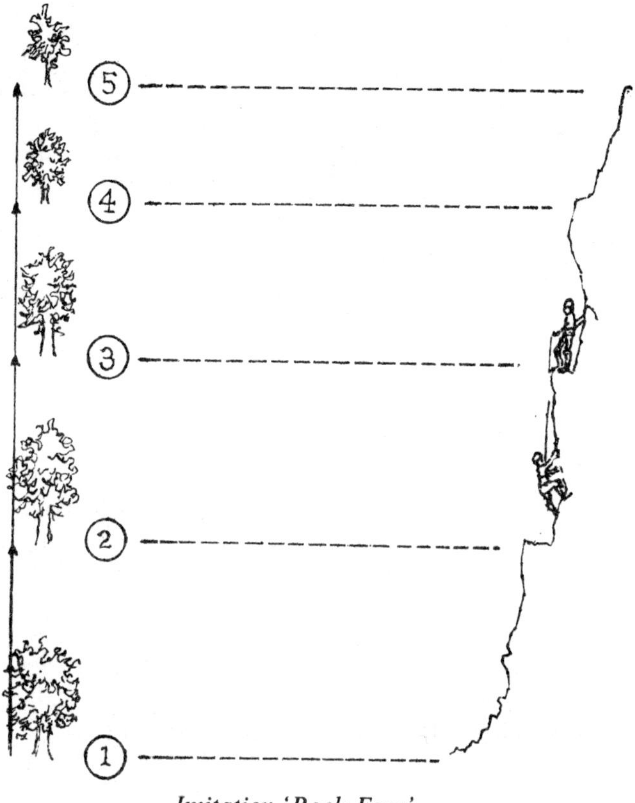

Imitation 'Rock Face'

ROPING UP

With a friend each tie on to the ends of this 'rope' with a figure of eight or double knotted bowline, finishing off with a 'tuck' knot and pulling the waistline nice and tight. You are now ready for climbing.

Belay at rock bottom

Think vertically from now on. Instead of horizontal ground stretching ahead from the first tree, you are standing at the base of a steep cliff. And either you or your partner is the leader who is going to climb up first to the first stance on the face – although actually this is the next tree in line; say about twenty yards away.

That leaves the other person as second man and he now belays to the first tree with the 'rope' – so he can't be torn away if the leader falls on the first pitch and goes bouncing down the hillside below. Well, say *you* are that second man. Use whichever belay is appropriate – a figure of eight, over a broken bough, or the other spike belay knot over a short branch or a thread belay around the whole trunk. Check the knots are right, the belay is tight to your waist and arrange the rope around your body as you would on a cliff.

First of all you must face outwards from the cliff rather than look towards it. So stand with your back to the tree trunk and looking out in the opposite direction from the line of trees behind you. Then loop the rope over your head and around the small of the back just above your belt. This forms a friction brake which helps to absorb the shock of a falling body – should the leader fall – through your own body. The diagram on page 83 will give you the idea (though this illustration also emphasis a key point about wearing the rope in a turn around one wrist, and which we deal with presently.)

Protecting the leader

Your companion, the leader, should begin to walk across to the first tree in line – slowly and stopping every foot or two as he would if it really was a rock face. And you, the second, pay out the rope around your back as he proceeds. The first difficulty a second experiences is paying out the rope efficiently – not too little nor too much. Pay out the rope too scantily and you will drag the leader back from his holds if he were to make a sudden movement upwards; pay out too generously and an arc or slack rope will develop which, if he fell, would mean the leader falls further than necessary before the rope can stop him.

At the first tree across the grass the leader has completed the equivalent of a rock face pitch, and he now gains the stance as he prepares to belay on the tree and bring you 'up' to him. After belaying he stands with his back to the tree just as on a cliff he would stand with his back to the rock – facing out and looking towards his second man. A stance? Remember? A ledge!

HOW THE LEADER BRINGS UP HIS SECOND MAN—AND THE CLIMBING CALLS

The leader takes in the rope to a sequence of belaying movements and shouts so that the second down below knows what is happening up above. These climbing 'calls' may seem ordinary in a park or field, but they are vital on a real crag when there may be as much as a hundred feet between two climbers who can no longer see each other and a wind is blowing away their yells. However, by calling a few terse pre-arranged words – as we shall see – the message gets through. Although the second man may only hear a faint word – 'IN', say – he then knows what is meant. In this case, that the leader has arrived safely on the stance above and is taking in the rope preparatory to bringing him up to join the leader.

Here is how it works

The leader pulls in the slack rope hand-over-hand shouting 'Taking in' as he starts hauling.

When the slack rope has all been taken in and the rope is now tugging on the second's waist, the second climber yells 'That's me'.

The leader loops the rope over his head and around his back (on a rock climb he will also take an extra turn of rope around one wrist, but we come to this later) and calls 'Climb when you're ready'.

The second removes his belay and shouts 'CLIMBING'. In this case, walking very slowly across the grass and stopping every foot or so on his way to join the leader. The leader replies by yelling 'Aye aye' or 'O.K.'

There are two more calls which are used when actually

climbing. If the leader is pulling too hard, the second shouts 'More rope'. But if the leader is not taking the rope in quickly enough the second calls 'Take in'. The ideal now, as you walk towards the leader, is for him to keep the 'rope' just taut enough to lift it clear from the ground without pulling hard on you.

You reach his stance and swap belays. This must be done carefully remember, for a real rock face stance could be a really small ledge indeed. To protect both of you during this change-over therefore the leader remains belayed and still holds the rope coming from your waist around his back while you belay to the same spike of branch or tree trunk. (If this is a spike belay slip the loop of rope up beneath the leaders belay and then tie it so that his belay still remains on top and can be removed when he is ready to climb without disturbing your own belay.) Now you are belayed and the leader can take the rope from his back. Facing back to the way you have just 'climbed' – out from the rock face, remember – you again take the rope around your back, so protecting the leader, he now takes his belay off and once again begins climbing on 'upwards' – across the grass to the third tree in line.

And so on from tree to tree, one at a time, until you both reach the last tree – stance after stance, pitch after pitch – which stands for the top of the climb, belaying each other all the way.

WHEN THERE ARE THREE CLIMBERS

Roping up is different for three climbers. When only one rope is used, the first and third climber tie on to each end with the figure of eight or double knotted bowline. And the second climber ties into the middle (double the rope first to locate this) with a figure of eight knot. On a real rock climb, however, two ropes will be used in most cases: leader and second tie to the ends of one rope and the last man ties to an end of the second rope. The other end of this rope is then tied to the second man's waistline with a figure of eight (repeat, round the second man's waistline, never round the second man's waist).

The sequence of climbing is a little different too. The leader goes first, the second follows, but now the third man also pays out the rope between him and the second man around his back to avoid snags in the rope pulling the second man back as he ascends.

If the stance above is large enough to hold all three climbers comfortably, the second climber brings up the third climber to join him and the leader. However, when the leader reaches a stance only big enough for him and his second, he brings up his second, and then climbs on up to the next stance above. Only when he reaches this further stance, has belayed and taken in the slack rope between himself and the second, does the second man then bring up the third man to his stance – and then climbs up to join his leader. The third man will join them if the stance above is big enough; if not, the same sequence applies as just described.

PRACTISING FALLS—AND HOW TO CHECK THEM

You need a pair of strong leather gloves to practise holding simulated falls during your 'climb' through the trees. You should also pad the lower part of your back from the fast-running 'rope' – wear an old jacket or extra couple of sweaters. This way you understand rope technique even better – especially after experiencing the stresses as the 'rope' goes as tight as a shark fisherman's line with a Great White on the far end.

HOLD A PLUNGING LEADER

Pay out the rope for the leader as he advances 'up' a pitch across the grass to a tree. Suddenly, mid-way, he yells, 'I'm off!' and turns to run towards you as you stand with your back towards him on the other side of your tree belay – the direction he would fall if he had slipped on the crag. Of course, he cannot stop at your belay but 'falls' on past just as would happen on the rock: . . . down . . . down to the second holding the rope . . . on down past him . . . down . . . until the rope finally stops him short.

As second man you now experience the terrific pull on your waist and on the belay which is holding you firm as the rope comes taut. The rope continues to slip fast round the back and through your fists, and you now know the reason for the gloves and padding for the waist. Gradually, however, you manage to bring the speeding 'rope' under control with the help of the friction of your body and stop the leader. You have had only an inkling of the terrific force generated by a falling climber, but you don't forget it.

HOLD A FALLING SECOND

It is now your turn to be leader and, having 'climbed' a pitch across the grass, you are belayed on a tree. Your second is approaching, and you take in the 'rope' as he 'climbs'. Suddenly he turns round the other way and starts to run back the way he has just come – in the direction he would fall were he on a face and suddenly 'lobbed off'. This too will be a shock on your body as you fight to brake it to a stop. But you manage it quite quickly and more easily than with the leader's longer and faster fall.

A falling second can usually be held in matter of inches because the rope was fairly taut to his waist anyway if not actually pulling on it. Seconds rarely fall far.

SAFEGUARDING THE LEADER

There are certain extra touches and precautions to make when handling ropes on a proper climb which can stop falls by either leader or second so much more efficiently.

PAY OUT THE LEADER'S ROPE IN GOOD TIME

NEVER drag the leader backwards as you – as second man – pay out his rope. It's a golden rule that cannot be stressed enough. It might not actually mean your slow rope handling plucks him bodily from his holds, but it could be enough to add that slight drag on the rope which upsets his critical balance as he steps up – and he falls.

If you are becoming flustered as you pay out the leader's rope: 1) ask him to slow down if possible on the easier climbing, and 2) pay out a foot or two of 'rope' in advance of the leader's movements so that you allow for any sudden jerk as he accelerates over a particularly crucial section without warning. You can make this a habit all the easier if you actually see the leader's progress. Do this by looking over a shoulder at him all the time, which is easier when you stand to the side of the tree on which he is climbing, and even though you have your back to it, take a half turn out from the 'crag' so that you can partly see the route he is taking.

Say your leader is 'climbing' above on your right hand side. Then face half right, back to the tree, and pay out the 'rope' through the right hand as shown – with the left hand in the 'dead' hand position; that is, feeding the slack rope up from the ground and round your back. This, basically, is exactly how you would pay out the rope on the rock face, and it is important that you get it right from the start.

TAKE THE CORRECT BRAKING POSITION

It is vital that the second is not dozing, but wide awake and alert if the leader should fall. He should be immediately ready to take the strain with both hands in front of the stomach, elbows tucked in tight, legs braced, especially the leg on the side of the 'rope' going to the leader which should be locked straight, leaning forward from the waist on the belay which is pulling tight at his waistline; ready to let the rope run at first but gradually checking it with the friction of the rope around his body and especially with the hand furthest away from the falling climber – the 'dead' hand.

But this is not nearly enough. You will find it takes all your time before you can halt a fast-running partner in his tracks. There is one more measure to take; always take it in future whenever you belay and pay out or take in your companion's rope.

HOW TO GAIN EXTRA STOPPING POWER WITH AN EXTRA TURN OF ROPE AROUND A WRIST

The following modification to paying out – or taking in – the rope should be something you always do from now on when belaying someone else – it was not mentioned earlier to avoid confusion.

Look on the hand which pays out – or takes in – your partner's rope as the 'live' hand. Look on the other hand which feeds up the rope from the slack coils on the ground as the 'dead' hand. And take an extra turn of your plastic clothes line around the wrist of the 'dead' hand as shown. You will find that this simple measure really does give you more power to the elbow in bringing a speeding rope to a stop. It won't be instant, but it will be far less gradual than with no turn of 'rope' at all round this wrist.

Second man pays out leader's rope

There is, however, one snag for beginners: this extra tactic will really slow down your rope handling and make you all fingers and thumbs again. So . . .

SPEED UP ROPE HANDLING WITH A SIMPLE DRILL

Practise for several minutes getting the hang of paying out the rope to the sequence described below and you will soon find that extra turn around the wrist is not the disadvantage it seems at first. In fact, you soon forget it's even there. And, most important, you never let go of the rope with either hand while paying it out.

Grip the rope by your hip with the 'live' hand and reach forward so drawing some rope forward at the same time.

Slide the 'dead' hand loosely along the rope coming into it from the slack coils on the ground – not gripping the rope in any way – then, keeping hold of the rope already in its loose grasp, also pinch the rope going out to the leader between finger and thumb just ahead of the 'live' hand.

Slip the 'live' hand back along the rope while the 'dead' hand remains in position as just described.

Repeat the whole sequence all over again – and again. It quickly becomes a natural motion.

The same problem of the turn around the 'dead' hand wrist slowing down the rope handling faces an inexperienced leader bringing up his second man, or a tryo second man fetching up a third climber. Yet the same drill is the answer, but in reverse. It is shown in this diagram.

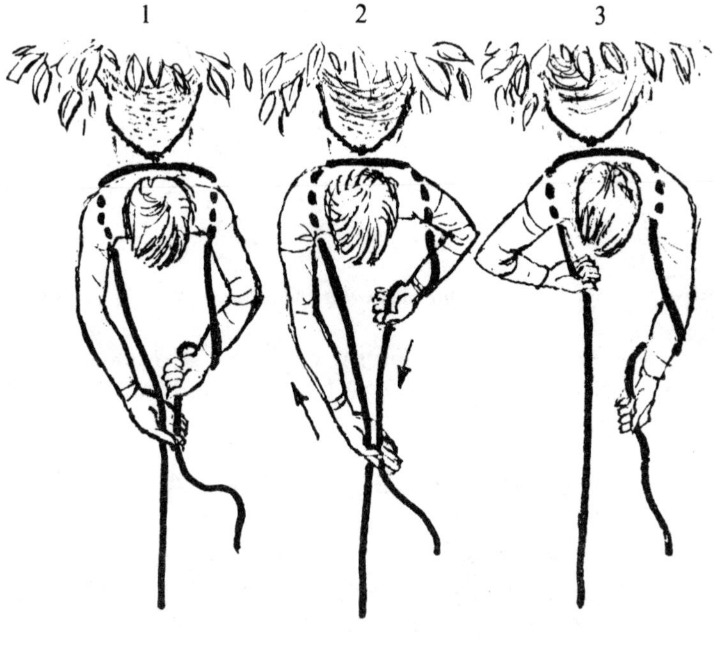

This time the 'dead' hand grasps the rope firmly and reaches forward so pulling some rope around the hips. The 'live' hand slips forward loosely along the rope coming straight up from the climber below, then also pinches the rope going down to the spare coils on the ground just in front of the 'dead' hand. The 'dead' hand slips back along the rope ready for repeating the sequence again and again.

HOW RUNNERS PROTECT THE LEADER

It will now be obvious that a falling leader is really vulnerable on a crag. He has so much further to fall if he slips. Especially on a long pitch. If he falls 50 feet above his second then he falls a distance of at least 100 feet in all – longer actually, as the rope stretches to absorb the shock and the leader can never stop the running rope dead in any case. He might, therefore, fall 130 feet or even 150 feet in the end. And the further he does fall, the more chance there is of the rope breaking through the sheer strain of a weight that grows heavier every foot extra it falls down the face – not to mention the higher chances of the rope fraying or cutting on some sharp rock edge far below.

Any measures which cut down the distance a leader has to fall are a priority therefore, and thankfully there is one: the running belay, or 'runner' for short. You can experiment with it now as the leader moves on from one tree to another.

PLACE A RUNNER AND CHECK A FALL

Before the leader 'climbs' a pitch to the next tree across the way he takes the sling mentioned earlier – that length cut off the plastic clothes line and used to hold your trousers up in the fisherman's knot experiment – and he clips the karabiner to this loop. Then he loops it over his head and a shoulder. Now he begins to walk, you paying out his rope.

On the way to the next tree he stops at the first obstacle on the ground which represents a spike on the rock face – such as a strong tree root, a big log, a piece of stone firmly embedded in the turf, a small tree or he actually bangs in a piece of strong stick into the ground and loops the sling over it. Then he clips the 'rope' through the karabiner and there you are – a safety pulley or runner.

Leaders using running belays

The function of the runner is made really obvious when, suddenly, the leader 'falls' and does his sprint back fast towards you. Not too fast, though! The sling and karabiner now act as that pulley and you quickly see just how effective this runner is in cutting down the distance the leader has to fall.

Providing the runner doesn't break or the anchor fracture, then a leader really is much safer – providing also that the second manages to hold the 'rope' as well. And, of course, on a proper rock face pitch the leader will place a number of runners so stitching himself to the rock at intervals. Leading thus becomes a calculated risk – and much less is left to chance for the man on the 'sharp end' than at first appears.

Collecting runners

As second man you must gather the runners left by the leader on each pitch of a rock climb. In the case of your tree 'climb' you have just the one runner to pick up as you walk across the grass to join your leader. It is easy to get into a knot here on a cliff while hanging one-handed to the rock, and to drop an expensive karabiner down the face while sorting out the sling.

Practise removing runners during your tree 'climb' therefore when there is no pressure on you. The easiest way when unsure is simply to lift the runner straight from its spike and loop it directly over your head. Do not unclip the karabiner until you reach either a resting place where you can use both hands in comfort or your leader's stance.

If you are in any doubt as to how the sling has been entwined round a chockstone or spike, first unclip the karabiner and place it in a pocket to avoid dropping it. Then attend to the sling. Only re-clip the karabiner back on to it when the sling is safely round your neck.

How to sort out a problem runner with a cat's cradle

Sometimes slings are extra long, and are worn doubled over the head and shoulder. When the anchor for a runner is extra large, however – a big chockstone or monster spike, say – then such a sling has to be unfurled so that its giant single loop can be wrapped around or over the particular jumbo-sized anchor concerned. This is fine for the leader who simply shakes out the doubled sling into one big loop and re-clips the karabiner over the single loop rather than over two loops, but it presents a problem for the inexperienced second. For he has to double the sling again and re-reclip the karabiner over both loops once more. (This re-reclipping of the karabiner is important since otherwise the sling develops into a tangle round the climber's body.) Easy enough, you might think, but wait. What actually happens is the sling is not doubled correctly by the novice – it only *looks* doubled – and the karabiner instead of being clipped on securely simply slides off the end as you are about to place the sling over your head.

When collecting a sling from a spike or chockstone which is too long to be worn as a single loop over your head and shoulder, double it – practise this now with any bit of string tied into a loop – to the following sequence.

Pull the loop out like a cat's cradle with a hand at each end both facing palm upwards and twist the loop once so the right hand is now palm downwards. Bring both hands together and place the end of the loop from the right hand into the left hand. The sling is now doubled correctly and to prove it . . . Clip the karabiner (or a large safety pin) to both loops. Drop one of the ends of the sling in the left hand, and the karabiner (or safety pin) will slide down and hang from that end.

And what of the wrong way of doubling the sling (so easily done)? Stretch out the loop between the hands palms up and – without crossing the loop – bring both hands together. Slip the end of the loop in the right hand into the left hand and you now have two separate loops dangling below. Clip these together with the karabiner and let go of one of the ends of the sling in your left hand. As the end falls the karabiner slides down the face).

SLINGS AS BELAYS

The comforting 'click' of the karabiner makes another key contribution to belaying technique, because you can belay to a spike or chockstone so much more quickly when you tie yourself to the anchor with a sling and karabiner instead of tying a belaying knot with the climbing rope. Try it now on one of the tree 'stances' of your 'climb' in the park.

Strap yourself to a crag

Arrange the sling around a branch or tree trunk either looped singly or doubled depending on the size of the anchor as shown in the diagram. Then clip the karabiner to your waistline – and

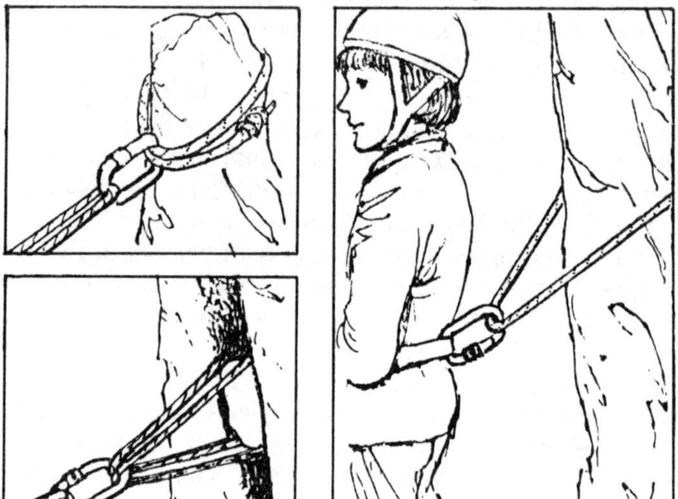

you are belayed. Always fix the sling by bringing the two ends together with the karabiner, incidentally – as shown – and avoid threading one end of the sling through the other as if to strangle the tree or chockstone concerned; it makes for a weaker anchor.

Convenient as belaying with a sling is compared to belaying with the climbing rope, beware of the dangers involved. Danger number one is, of course, that slings are usually of thinner rope than the climbing rope itself and therefore weaker. When belaying – climbers consequently use more than one sling where possible; over as many small nicks and notches as they can find which will support sling belays, but which would be too diminutive to accommodate the thick climbing rope. Another danger is in the use of karabiners which have inherent dangers: they can fail mechanically (rare) or through human failure (not quite as rare). We will come to this in a moment.

Using both sling and rope for belaying

Say the only anchor at a stance is a spike several feet above your head. Rather than climb up and drape the rope over it, then come down and struggle to adjust your belay knot – it is a struggle because of the friction involved when you try to pull the rope over the sharp edges of the spike to gain that final adjustment – simply place a sling, preferably doubled, over the spike and belay into the karabiner with a figure of eight loop or spike belay knot as previously explained. Adjust the belay to come tautly to your waist.

This combined use of sling and rope belay can be used in a number of ways. Try them on your trees 'climb' – the obvious example here being thread belays where the sling is wrapped around a branch a foot or two above your head and then the 'rope' is clipped into the karabiner as just explained with a figure of eight or spike belay.

Avoid deadly karabiner errors

A karabiner can fail, when a climber falls and it is subjected to a sudden shock loading through metal fatigue or some other flaw, but a more common cause of failure is when a climber is careless. Here are three such dangers.

One is where an ordinary karabiner without a locking sleeve on its gate is used and the gate faces uppermost – should the climbing rope accidentally jam the gate open with the now present risk that the karabiner can slip off the waistline altogether as the body of the belayed climber twists and turns under the shock of a falling companion. The second danger is when, as has happened, *two* such ordinary karabiners have been used to link a climber to a sling belay. The karabiners lie across each other while the climber is standing relaxed, his belay drooping slackly behind him, only to jerk against each other and lever themselves apart during the sudden violent wrench as the other climber falls and the load comes on the belay without warning. The third danger is when a karabiner attaches a climber to his sling belay with the gate facing the ground – only for a sudden fall by his companion to pull the belayed climber sharply in one direction where the karabiner gate is brought sharply against an edge of rock which forces it open and off the waistline or climbing belt altogether. And these are only three such instances – there have been other similar cases too.

Make it a rule, therefore, only to belay direct to a sling belay with a screw-gated karabiner – like the type I suggested you buy before starting this chapter. And constantly keep checking to see that the gate is, in fact, kept locked (an edge of rock, for example, could be rubbing against the karabiner as you pay out the rope and this could twist the sleeve locking the gate free without your knowing).

When you must belay with an ordinary non-locking karabiner – the screw-gated karabiners are being used elsewhere on your climb, say – then turn the karabiner so that gate always faces the ground and keep checking that no part of the rock can force the gate open while your attention is kept on handling the rope. An extra safeguard is to use two ordinary karabiners attaching you to a sling belay, one with the gate facing upwards, the other with the gate facing down. Even these don't guarantee perfect safety, however; keep checking them as you pay out – or take in – the rope. Having respect for karabiners – and of their possible weaknesses – is a key step to later climbs where you quite possibly use one of the various 'mechanical' belaying systems like the sticht plate.

6 Snow Slope Basics

The complete climber must be able to get to grips with snow and ice as well as rock – not so much as an alpinist heading for an ice climb either, but as someone walking along a mountain track and suddenly meeting snow slopes. It is now that all-round experience counts most when hard-frozen snow might look easy-angled but, in fact, is so deceptively steep. And a slip would have you tumbling for hundreds of feet down the hill-side.

Crampons make a world of difference – like something from a *Captain Marvel* comic, in fact. Strap them to your boots and – Wow! – it is possible to claw a way up the steepest ice simply by pressing them against the face. Powered by the legs, the climber has no longer any need to hack out a painstaking stair-case of footholds up the ice first with his ice axe, always a tiring and time-consuming business. However, as with using 'power' tools of any kind, it pays to have mastered the rudiments of hand tools first. Buckling on crampons for your first outing is akin to chopping down a tree – your first ever – with a chain-saw. The trunk topples on top of your bicycle or whatever is beneath, because you overlooked the most basic rules in your effort to concentrate on the mechanical aspects of the tool itself. It's the same with crampons. You first need to experi-ence to climb up snow and ice by actually chopping into it with the ice axe, then you know what to expect when the time comes to don crampons later.

You must also learn to handle an ice axe as a brake if you fall; the only way a plunging climber can stop on his own. But try it the first time wearing crampons and – problems! Those very points which make it such a pleasure to climb when used properly can dig into the slope and tip you head over hills as you tumble downhill, and so your fall becomes uncontrollable. Learn without this extra complication first on local snow slopes therefore.

Make the most of snow while it lasts and be adaptable. Soft snow, for example, is a drag, but only if you let it be. There seems to be no way of making fast slides, an exciting way of learning to get the 'feel' of steep snow, for example – just one activity you can do. There are no thrills and spills – it's all a bit disappointing. Not to worry. Remember Scott at the South Pole whose reaction on at last reaching it was: 'My God, what a dreadful place.' And make the best of existing conditions by carefully converting that soft snow into a surface as hard and smooth as glass. It takes more effort, but is worth it. First, though, you need ice axes.

YOUR OWN ICE AXE FACTORY

As with bouldering experiments already described in Chapter 4, snow slope trials are best done with a group. It's safer and more fun. Now it is unrealistic to expect everyone, indeed anyone, to own a proper ice axe costing at least £12 at this stage – although on a mountain they are vital. There are ways, however, of improvising 'ice axes' for each person in the group.

You can simulate nice short-ish modern ice axes by cutting short sections of strong tree branch – around 65cm to 75cm – in the shape shown in the illustration. An inch or two from the end of each branch should sprout a short length of branch –

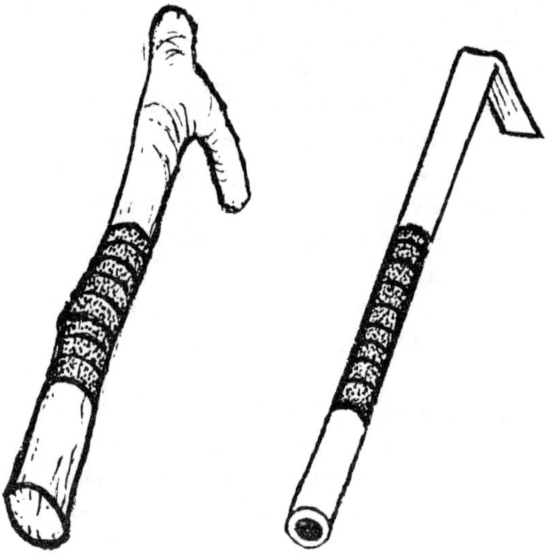

also strong – jutting back down like the spout of a soda siphon. This is the 'pick' as shown in the diagram in Chapter 2. Look for such 'ice axes' carefully and selectively; on no account go ripping branches from trees haphazardly. Then cut them off with a small saw or penknife. The handle of each 'axe', incidentally, must be smooth and fit into your fists so your thumbs can just encircle the wood as you grasp it. Alternatively a similar length of strong metal pipe of the same diameter can also be 'bent' into an ice axe shape – a rough one, true, but effective— after hammering the 'pick' end flat. Wrap insulating tape round wood or metal handle to improve the grip.

Carrying the ice axe

Although a tree branch or metal pipe 'ice axe' may seem devoid of points, a proper ice axe is anything but. Carried the wrong way it can be a dangerous weapon. In the first instance, you must know how to attach it to a climbing rucksack – as in the diagram in Chapter 2.

The axe is slipped spike first down through the small loop at the base of the rucksack, then the shaft is tilted out and back upwards to be strapped in position against the front of the sack as shown. One snag, however: the axe will tilt out somewhat at an angle when, for instance, the climber is running downhill. To someone immediately behind there is a risk if the front man was to stop suddenly. So watch out.

HOW TO BOMB DOWN SNOW

The ice axe priority is stopping falls downhill with it. It's all too easy falling on a slog up or across what *looked* like an easy snowfield . . . But footholds are glassy and – SKID! Footholds here are also frail and – SNAP! Then, tumbling down a mountain, only you and you alone can stop the headlong flight. More power to your elbows (and arms and fists) controlling your 'ice axe' therefore if you have first shot down safe trial slopes so fast your hair is windblown enough to break off the teeth in your comb as you try to sort it out afterwards. (Watch it, though: you should be wearing a crash hat of some description as stressed in Chapter 2 – yes, even in practise.) This way you learn to control dangerous skids on your own skid pan at home.

Snow slides

If local slopes are hard frozen there is no problem. Your braking trials will be fast enough. But what about mushy, thawing or even newly fallen snow where it seems impossible to pick up speed as you try to bomb downhill? The answer is to make a slide. And not just one but several. Then you can use them in rotation before they begin to show too many signs of wear and tear.

Slides can be found in playgrounds, streets, backyards and parks – anywhere young people gather on snow. Just follow the shrieks and laughter to the stretch of snow which has been gang-polished with shoe leather until it is a strip of gleaming glass anything from five to 30 yards long. Sliders take a run, jump on, fly along its icy surface, arms wildly semaphoring to keep in balance, then leap or fall off at the bottom depending on agility.

Make a number of such slides on the steepest little slopes you can find on a heath, in a park or among woods and fields. There should be a clear run-out at the bottom – no walls, no fences – and be free from hazard like rocks, trees and barbed wire in the snow on the way down.

Now, the harder the snow the faster you will slide. Great! If you find you are going so fast your eyes water – ideal! With soft snow, however, the surface needs compacting first, then burnishing over and again with repeated descents to make it really skiddy.

Tin trays are fine for moulding such slides from scratch. So are plastic washing up bowls and flat dustbin lids. Grease them with candlewax or even banana skins as was once used to grease runways for ships in the olden days. Sit, feet up, on such a 'sledge' and skim down the same path over and over again until you wear it into a shallow groove. Bank up bare spots with more soft snow, then tamp it down firmly with the flat of a shovel. Don't allow other toboggans or pedestrians to cross the path of a slide or they will spoil the surface. Also sprinkle the snow with a watering can last thing before going home when frost is in the air.

Glissading

Glissading is great fun in a field or a park, but can be dangerous on mountains. Speed is the reason. It's like ski-ing without skis. And while local snow slopes are the equivalent of safe nursery slopes, mountain slopes pose hazards like cliffs unseen when you approach from above . . . not to mention patches of iron-hard ice, scree and boulders and a much greater distance to slide if you ever were to lose control. Remember this therefore. Glissade now for practise. *Forget about glissading on mountains, however.*

Glissading is valid training because it teaches you stand tall on steep snow. And standing balanced on your own two feet thus is as important for an alpinist as for a gunfighter. It also instils in you how to be quick on the draw with your ice axe. All you need, then, are wellingtons or leather-soled shoes – something that will skid downhill really easily – and your homemade 'ice axe'. Incidentally, your slide should not be too hard-surfaced for this technique.

Stand on the edge of your slide – feet together and pressed down flat and holding the 'ice axe' across your body. The pick should be pointing down at the snow, held in the right hand (if you are right-handed) with thumb and forefinger hooked around the main length of branch just above the 'pick'. (Or, if using a proper ice axe, around the neck of the axe head just below the wide part of the adze ' see the illustration in Chapter 2.) Your left hand grasps the 'handle' down towards the 'spike'.

Push the toe of one boot or shoe just ahead of the other. If you now point the toes downwards a little, and your slide is really glassy, you will start to slide. To keep in balance trail the left hand end – the 'spike' end – of your 'ice axe' lightly on the snow. As you gain speed, however, you can press it down for control. Flex the knees and keep your weight right over the leading boot. You can now begin to turn in zig zags. Simply push the other boot forwards instead and transfer your weight.

How fast you go depends on side slipping with the body and digging the edges of your boots into the snow. Not only do you slew the boot soles parallel to the slope, but by turning them up or down like the wing flaps of a Jumbo jet you can apply the anchors – especially as snow can pile up beneath to act as a shock-absorber. Dig in the spike end of the axe, too.

By leaning out on the 'ice axe' like a canoeist on his paddle you will be able to steer, as you swap the 'axe' over from side to side, depending on which direction you wish to take. This applies especially to firm snow where you can glide over any part of the surface rather than in soft snow conditions where you are restricted to the straight downhill groove of your slide. If you fall, however, and the slope is so steep that you carry on speeding downhill you will be able to stop yourself quickly by practising the experiments listed below.

Make a superslide

A superslide is wider and longer. It must be steeper, too, or you gain the wrong impression of mountain slope conditions. You want, in fact, the kind of slope which makes a helter skelter toboggan run where you go like the wind. And tobogganing is exactly the thing to compact soft snow into a glassy groove for your experiments. Best way: sit in a plastic speed-bob sledge – the kind sold in supermarkets – and slide repeatedly down the same channel until it is glassy and fast. (Toboggans with old-fashioned runners, however, are useless for making super slides compared with flat-bottomed sledges.) Make several such Crestas.

Plastic bag sledging

No speed-bob? Then obtain a strong polythene bag from a garden shop large enough to climb into, and then pull up to your chest. Lay it flat out on top of the slope, then take a run and belly-flop your way downhill Cresta run-style, grasping the front two corners of the bag in your fists, and keeping both feet up off the snow. Although polythene sheeting slides very fast, it doesn't skim as far as a heavier toboggan unless its path is smoothed out first ahead. First time down, therefore, extend your superslide by 'paddling' the plastic sheet along with the hands as it begins to slow down on the easy incline at the bottom. Dig the fingers into the snow on either side and push your way down and across the run-out – rather as if lying on an air mattress and paddling it across a swimming pool.

You will find that once you have laid out the foundation for the slide in this way, the plastic sheet sled will faithfully follow this faint groove and the more slides you make down it the more hair-raising it becomes! If, however, the sled veers off at any time and makes a new 'branch line' as it were, cancel this out by dumping soft snow on the point of departure from the straight and narrow – on the point where sled left the tracks. Flatten it down to follow the shape of the superlide's channel. Everything is now ready for braking trials.

First, however, race your sled. It's fun to compete for the fastest times against other tobogganists either down the one slide – you use a wristwatch – or by racing down several slides all together from a mass start. The important thing is that racing makes you travel all the faster – and that makes the following experiments all the more realistic.

How to stop

'Burning off' the opposition as you swoop downhill to race your rivals is one thing. Applying the anchors with the ice axe when it seems you can never stop, however, is quite another. At first it seems impossible. Well, remember, that a high percentage of mountain accidents – as much as 25 per cent in areas where snow and ice are found for several months each year – are caused by the lack of an ice axe or the inability to use an ice axe to stop falls on slopes of hard snow. And be quite determined you personally are never going to be so caught out.

The best way to practise ice axe self-arrest is by climbing into your large polythene bag and drawing it up to the armpits like a sleeping bag. Wearing a nylon parka, anorak or cagoule also helps as such a slippery garment will help boost your speed. And wear some form of crash helmet. You then take your 'ice axe', go to the top of a superslide and carry out these test runs.

Sitting down

Sit on top of the superslide, feet pointing down it as if on a toboggan. Hold your 'ice axe' across your body in the grip detailed in the glissading experiment – 'pick' pointing down, right thumb and forefinger hooked around the length of handle just above the 'pick' and other hand grasping the far end of the handle.

Push yourself off – or get a friend to push you. Wait until you gather speed. Then, to stop: lie back down on the slope and, throwing your left leg across as far as it will move inside the plastic bag, roll over to the right on to your chest – it must be to the right as the head of the axe is in your right hand and this is the part of the axe you use as brake (roll over to the left instead, however, and the spike end of the 'axe' would catch in the snow and wrench the handle out of your clutch). Keeping the head of the 'axe' near your right shoulder, tuck both elbows firmly into the side and press the 'pick' into the snow with your body weight and chest across the handle. Only do it gradually with increasing pressure. Too abrupt a jabbing in of the pick – what with the combination of your weight forcing down and the 'pick' just entering the snow (especially when icy) – can rip the 'ice axe' from your grasp. This must never happen. Indeed the value of a fast superslide is that it instils in you the instinct to hang on to this vital survival tool by using correct technique from the start.

Belly-flops

Just as you first slid downhill on your polythene bag sled head-first and on your front, do the same now inside the plastic bag, axe across your body and held clear of the snow until you have hit top speed. The diagram shows you how. Pad the adze with rags if you are using a real ice axe to protect any accidental blow to your face. And as you accelerate down the slide watch the axe pick with all the concentration of a batsman facing a pace bowler. (The bag isn't shown for clarity).

Again, apply gradual pressure as you press the pick into the slope. You should reach well out to the right to do this. Tuck the elbows in and as the pick begins to bite, let the legs swing round in an arc until they are pointing downhill. You can now begin to bring your whole body weight on to the pick to drive it into the snow as you roll over until lying on top of the snow.

There are two final hints to aid better braking. One you cannot really do inside your plastic bag, and that is *really* throw your left leg across as you roll onto the snow and then, as you apply the 'pick', keep the legs wide apart. The bag itself

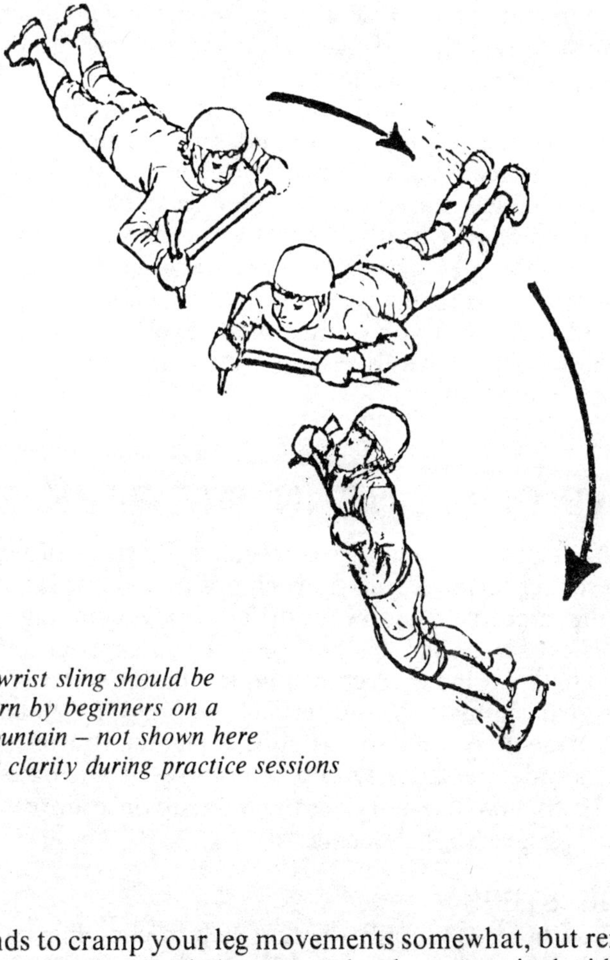

A wrist sling should be worn by beginners on a mountain – not shown here for clarity during practice sessions

tends to cramp your leg movements somewhat, but remember once past the plastic bag stage that legs apart is the ideal. The other concerns the elbow of your arm applying the pick. It is by using this as a kind of fulcrum that you can best apply gradual pressure when braking. At first the elbow takes most of your weight, then the pick takes over as you apply more and more weight to it.

There are other positions from which to practise braking like sliding downhill on your back looking up and also somersaulting downwards in a forward roll, then bringing yourself to a sudden halt. These call for a certain amount of nerve, agility and confidence and it is safest if you leave these alone until you are with an experienced climber on snow slopes. You can then, if so inclined, do the more advanced twists and rolls under his supervision and with less risk to injuring yourself.

Self-arrest practice ploughs up slides very quickly – the reason why you really need a number of slides is so that you can ring the changes. Pack the ruts and holes in the snow with more snow and press firmly down with a shovel. Then, to renew the former glassiness which will keep up your speed, makes several tobogganing trips downhill again on your plastic bag sled or a speed bob (minus the axe, of course) to get back in the groove again as it were.

ALPINE CLIMBING IN THE PARK

If learning the ropes among trees revealed the roots of basic climbing sequence, practising snow climbs up a toboggan run will – by the same token – show the drift of winter climbing tactics too. Hard-frozen snow is best so that you experience the support given by using correct technique – unlike softer snow where you can simulate the proper method but don't actually 'feel' any benefit. When snow is soft, I suggest you use old snow slides and superslides. Dump more snow on bare patches and tread it down well. Then gloss the slides up once more with plastic sled or speed-bob descents.

KICKING STEPS

Kicking footholds is literally the first step in climbing snow. Wear the boots recommended in Chapter 2, a nylon anorak, parka or cagoule or even a plastic mac (even now you will still need to check falls with the ice axe, and the faster these garments help you slide the better!) and carry your 'ice axe'. Just how you grasp this is very important . . .

Pull a friend from his holds

This most basic exercise of taking a climber by surprise will ensure he learns always to grasp his ice axe correctly as he kicks steps up, down or across steep snow. It is a fundamental behind all snow and ice climbing.

The 'climber' simply ties the length of plastic clothes line – used in Chapter 5 – around his waist so that the rest of the line dangles down the front between his legs as he climbs. Then, as he kicks his steps up a snow slide or snowdrift – and after towing out a good amount of line behind him as he climbs above and to one side of you – take a turn of this 'rope' around a fist and pull sharply backwards like they do in the films with a steel wire to the recipient of a Colt .45 bullet. The falls in both cases are more realistic because of the sudden jerk. In your friend's case, however, he will save himself with practise.

By using (as he climbs):

(1) THE REST STEP. Use the ice axe as a third leg while holding it like a walking stick, the uphill hand on top and pick always pointing behind (reason in a moment). The sequence goes like: axe in . . . left boot . . . right boot . . . axe out . . . axe in . . . left boot . . . and so on. So there is always two points of contact on steep snow and added stability at each move.
(2) THE SAFETY HANDLE. If footholds crumble on softish snow . . . Simply push the axe handle straight into the snow and hang on to the head which you were grasping anyway as you climbed. So you check yourself at once.
(3) THE SELF-ARREST. When the snow is too hard to admit the axe handle as above, a sudden fall is still quickly stopped with the axe pick – as described earlier – as you actually fall downhill.

Because the pick is already pointing towards the rear the axe can immediately be brought across the body – other hand reaching for the spike end – and the adze brought up to the shoulder in one movement. Try it to see just how easy it is to brake this way when the unexpected happens (but if the adze was facing to the rear you would waste time first having to turn the axe around).

How snowballs trip you

Another reason for suddenly falling without warning while kicking steps – natural this time – is the build-up of snow beneath your boot soles when the slopes are soft. Try tramping about in your commando soled boots across freshly fallen snow or melting snow and it becomes obvious. To avoid these 'platform' soles forming keep lightly tapping the sides of your boots with the spike end of the axe handle as you climb.

Footplacing under stress

Kicking steps – simple as it may seem after the precision footwork needed for bouldering – can be as difficult a technique to do properly as trapping a football in a tense goalmouth melee. So make it tough on yourself now – and learn. Pack your duffle bag rucksack with books or stones (pad down the back inside the 'sack' with a sweater for comfort). Or tie the plastic clothes line around your waist and tow a large polythene bag full of snow some way behind you up a glassy snow slide. You must now place both feet correctly or you will overbalance under the extra load and fall.

Aim for one kick per foothold. Try not to use conscious effort either. Just let the leg's swing and boot's weight dent the slope sufficiently enough to make a small foothold. As the boot lands, incidentally, press it down with a little jab to help compact the step. It helps to keep the boot soles perfectly level and to face the slope so that you kick steps straight uphill when the angle allows.

Kick a diagonal line of steps up and across steep snow, however. Use the inner and outer edges of the boots so the rubber teeth of your commando soles can actually saw through the ice crystals at a kick. Again, keep the boots level. And don't kick steps too far apart as it takes more effort to lift the legs repeatedly high. On steep soft snow it's best to kick double steps side by side so spreading your weight more evenly and giving the footholds less chance of breaking under your weight.

The ice axe as support

When the slope becomes steeper the walking stick ice axe grip becomes less of an aid. There are two other positions of holding the axe, however, which actually brace you on the snow. (There are even more ways of gripping the axe than these, too, but the following pair are standbys whenever you are on mountains.)

The 'prop'

Hold the ice axe horizontally across your body when traversing or climbing diagonally, with the pick held pointing downhill in the outer fist which grips the narrow neck of the adze – and the other hand holding the spike end of the handle against the snow. You can now balance upright on your footholds instead of tending to 'lie' against the slope. Any slip can be checked at once, the axe being already in the self-arrest position if you fall, and the spike acting as the prop to prevent this happening in the first place – just jab it in. Only do it to the right sequence where the inside foot (to the slope) always leads off; axe in . . . left boot (if traversing to the right) . . . right boot . . . axe out . . . axe in . . . left boot . . . and so on.

The 'sky hook'

The axe is held in the self-arrest position diagonally across your chest when negotiating really steep slopes, but you press the pick (or adze this time if the surface of the snow is crusted with softer snow beneath) into the slope well above your head and actually pull on it for stability.

Descend under stress

Carrying a full rucksack, or towing a loaded polythene bag attached to you by line from below will help make any descent down a steep little slope – yes, even a toboggan run – more realistic. Descend kicking steps facing out and digging in the heels – straight-legged. Keep your weight straight above your boots, keep your toes up and keep your ice axe grasped across the body – pick down, of course – ready for braking if you fall. For steeper slopes, however, you need to back your way down facing in as you kick steps with the toes and hold the ice axe in the 'skyhook' position as detailed above.

CUTTING STEPS

When snow becomes frozen too hard to kick steps with just the one kick, you must cut steps with the ice axe – at least until you have graduated on easy winter climbs to the crampon-wearing stage. There are snags here as far as your experiments around home go. Your tree branch 'axe' will not really be suitable. You may well be hard put to it finding snow deep enough and sufficiently hard for decent practise. And although it is possible to chop steps in the small snowdrifts available, many young people find this boring without a proper ice axe and without any real height to gain. Best thing then is for us to treat step cutting *very* basically until you have bought or borrowed an ice axe and can practise under supervision on mountain snow slopes.

'Pulling' footholds

There's no question of yanking a friend from his holds here. Now it's the footholds themselves which you 'pull'. Do it like this: cut small steps one-handed (not two-fisted) and stand balanced straight up on them. Slash at the snow, keeping the shoulder in the same position without the body; and aim to cut one step with each stroke. A proper ice axe is heavy enough to aid you by its weight and your arm swing alone. A home-made axe, however, needs more muscle. Lean on steeper snow with the inner hand and 'pull' each step with the outer.

Good, firm snow is easy to cut simply by raking the bottom corner of the adze (or the bent bit of your wooden branch or metal pipe axe) across towards you. Six inches is enough. Then step upon such a slash in the snow with the inside edge of your boot – pressing down to make the hold dip in a little towards the slope. It takes practice to find just the right angle to take or 'pull' the snow; otherwise the adze bounces off or simply digs in and sticks fast. Bigger side steps which will accommodate a complete boot sole are made on the same principle – but by a series of 'pulls'. First kick across the snow with the inside edge of your boot. Then cut two or three times along the kick mark to peel away your snow chunks. The little ledge should slope steeply inwards.

These are the basics. The sequence of cutting steps – in single or double series, diagonally across or straight up and down – is best left for now, however, until you are on longer snow slopes and under proper supervision.

Cutting steps up. . . .

and down

BELAYING ON SNOW

Snow and ice climbing sequence is the same as for rock – as practised in Chapter 5. A big difference between rock and snow and ice climbing, however, is the great difficulty in finding reliable belays on snow and ice. Although rock belays should be used wherever possible, there will be many times when you must use the snow itself for anchorage. For now, therefore, let's test the main kind of belay on any nearby snowdrift.

Try to disturb a dead man

You need a snowdrift by and preferably reaching a height of several feet above a quiet road or car park, and a friendly owner's car. If none of these are available any snowdrift will do, and you supply the power for this experimental rig with a tug of war team.

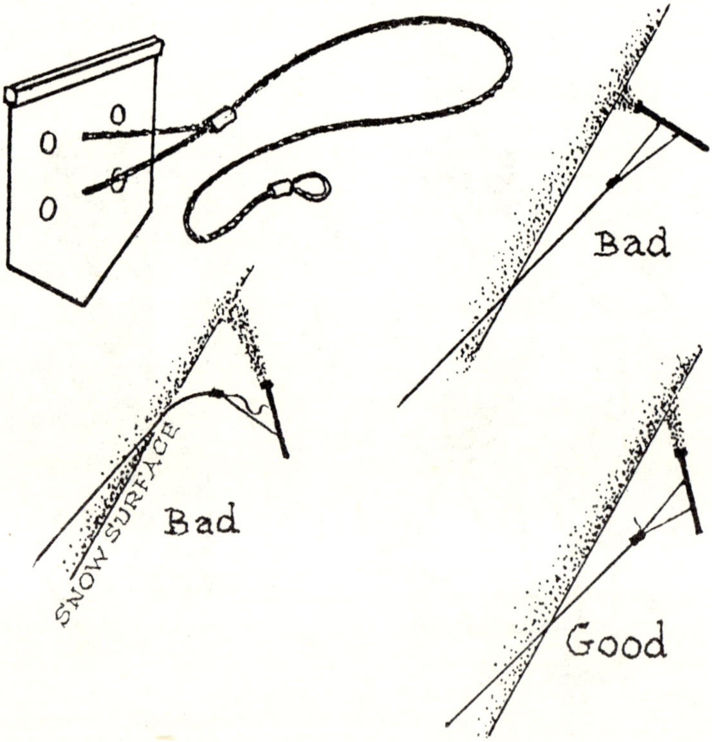

Cut a dead man to the approximate dimensions shown from thick plywood, an old flat shovel or anything similar. Drill two holes through the centre and pass a length of strong rope through which you then knot with a bowline and leave a tail of not less than 6ft long – its end being tied with a small figure of eight. Clip your karabiner into this, find your snowdrift and . . .

Carve two *deep* slits in the snow to form a 'T'. Place the dead man down inside the shorter topmost slot at least a foot deep, then lead the rope tail down the other slit. Be careful to place the dead man at the correct angle first, though. (To estimate: *hold your 'ice axe' at 90° to the slope just over the slot, then halve the angle on the uphill side with the dead man so it leans at 45° ; now tilt it back a further 5° and push it down.*) Only if the snow is wet or powdery should you stamp it down – otherwise place it by hand. And avoid trampling the snow beneath the long downhill slot – another way of weakening snow in certain conditions. Now draw the long rope tail straight down through the long slit making sure it comes down at the correct angle as shown; otherwise a sudden strain on the rope could flip the dead man up into the air. (A proper dead man has a wire rather than rope sling and this works as a cheesecutter actually knifing through the snow and settling into the correct position on its own accord.) Pull hard down on the sling. Does it seem straight, feel firm? If sited properly the buried plate will settle in further. But now is the time to tell . . .

Attach a car tow rope to the karabiner with a figure of eight knot and the other end to the car. The driver should now put the car into first gear and drive away. A properly placed dead man will bite further into the snow and either the tow rope breaks or the car's back wheels spin so much it is unable to gain traction and move. (This anchor was, after all, first used to tether husky teams in Antarctica.) But it must be properly placed.

How shovelling the path shows the secret

The dead man when under pressure moves down and compresses the snow below it. In bad soft snow a dead man may move several feet when it comes under a sudden pull – then it sticks fast. Clearing snow from the garden path? Try holding the shovel vertical and pushing the snow along in front of it. It's soon no-go because the snow piles up into a hard unyielding mass – the dead man at work!!

Other snow and ice belays

Snow conditions are ever-changing on mountains and the dead man is the only anchor which can be used in all of them – except, naturally enough, ice. For ice you need to hack out a mushroom-shaped bollard which takes time or use ice screws, which also require some expertise. There are also ways of belaying with the ice axe which are notoriously unreliable unless done expertly as this tool was not designed for belaying. For the moment, become accustomed to the dead man from the very start as the only reliable anchor on snow and this even second in preference to a good rock belay wherever you can find one among snow and ice.

Unseat a friend from a bucking tea tray

You can test just how a dead man works on a climb – be it the North Wall of the Eiger or the South-West Face of Everest – on any steep and fast toboggan run which has a snowdrift just to one side of the steepest section about 20 feet beneath the top. Station yourself in the snowdrift by cutting a stance into it with a shovel (on the mountain you would use a proper ice axe). This must be a solid flat ledge cut with care. Then place your dead man in the drift at least 10 feet above.

Tie around your waist one end of your plastic clothes line, or preferably a stronger rope – remembering that, of course, this experiment *must only be conducted in a field or somewhere similar and never on a large hill or mountainside.* Attach the other end through the hole punched in the edge of a tin tea tray.

Your companion takes the tea tray to the top of the slope and sits on it, his 'ice axe' held across his body in the self-arrest position, his feet – for the moment – on the snow, the tray turned so that the 'rope' is fastened to it at the back. You, meanwhile, reach up and belay to the dead man – as the drawing shows – with a figure of eight knot into the karabiner. Make sure the belay is nice and taut to your waist. Then pull on gloves (leather-palmed ones are best), and loop the 'rope' over your head and around your back – taking it round the furthest

wrist away from the toboggan run too – in approved belaying fashion. You now have an *indirect belay* to the dead man, and the 'rope' comes down to your hands from the tea tray with a little extra slack to spare. You should be wearing most of your sweaters and anorak or cut-down mac for padding against the fast-running 'rope' too. Fast-running what? Well, everything is pretty well static right now, but watch out when – at a pre-arranged signal – your pal launches himself off and, feet up, hurtles down the slope towards and past you to the side.

Just as you fielded a falling leader in Chapter 5 among the trees, so you brace your leg nearest the slide and bring both arms across your body to increase the friction on the 'rope'. If you can stop the tea tray within a foot or two so that your friend is unseated and carries on shooting down the slope on his back side – great! (He has his 'ice axe' if he needs to stop.) It's a good exercise in experiencing the real thing. Only it will take a little time for you to get everything right. And if, instead, your friend actually sticks it out and rides the bucking tea tray and as a result the 'rope' breaks or the snow surrounding the dead man collapses around you and you are pulled off the stance too . . . Well, as you pick yourself up out of the snow at the bottom of the slope, put it all down to experience and thank your lucky stars you didn't first come across this situation of a belay failing high on a mountain. Find out where you went wrong and try again.

FINAL REMINDER

Slides and skid pans near home can only simulate the real thing. Mountains thick with snow and ice are a vastly different proposition. There, it is absolutely necessary that you visit even their lower slopes for practise with a competent climber. And that in reaching for the top on winter walks, you should be fully equipped with ice axe, warm clothing, a rope, emergency supplies and a party of preferably four to six people. Unfortunately such precautions are only too frequently neglected by young climbers in the rush to reach snow covered mountains while winter conditions last. It is very difficult to resist this urge when you have bought a brand-new ice axe and other winter climbing gear – even though you are short on experience. Yet it is most important that you do – and show restraint, too, as when this chapter suggests you go out to train on local toboggan slopes and snowdrifts in 'safe' surrounds.

Snow and ice, remember, are so much more an unpredictable a climbing surface than rock. Rock, after all, is 'rock solid', but the underlying layers of snow beneath the surface – affected by previous days of wind, sun, rain and frost – can offer as much danger as an unexploded minefield without your ever realising it. And whereas on a rock climb the occasional handhold might snap off, on snow a whole great slab might avalanche, or you might lose your footing on what appeared to be a perfect surface because the snow was not all it looked.

Stress to yourself, finally, then, the importance of your ice axe. Never forget it. This essential accessory which, quite apart from its use as prop and step-cutter, above all else provides the disc brakes should you ever tumble down snow and ice. Without it you are helpless. Practise braking with the ice axe at any good opportunity and, need I say it, never drop it by accident.

7 First Real Climbs

The first 'real' climbs are always those, whether you had already been through a climbing course, or simply taken up a rock face route behind a climber who offered to take you along – which you tackle with a friend who probably knows as little as you. And with no help from anyone else. It's the two of you together AND the crag – factors which are very different from being taken in tow by an instructor. 'That *was* real,' you say at the top, because now it's your own effort and judgment which has proved up to the task, ensured you survived and also, most important of all, that you enjoyed the experience. If you constantly frighten yourself on early rock climbs you are in danger. You are trying climbs that are really too difficult for you. And that can be fatal. Let's take this final chapter, then, through the safest stages which leads to those first 'real' climbs – the break-through for YOU.

HOW TO FIND SOMEONE WHO WILL TAKE YOU CLIMBING

The safest introduction to a rock face is when your hands shake while reaching for its handholds – and an expert has you fastened to the rope he is handling from above. Everything you have practised at home is now put into use, and he will tell you what you are doing wrong – any untidy or risky habits unchecked during your early backyard bouldering sessions. Rock face exposure too – all that thin air! – can be most unnerving to the tyro, no matter how much training has left his fingerprints on door lintels and window sills near ground-level. Yet having that rope tied round the waist and knowing an ace is handling it up above is a steadying experience; you are in no danger and any fall is checked within inches. This is the way most people learn to climb. It is certainly one most parents go along with.

Climbing courses

The Sports Council, 70 Brompton Road, London SW3, runs climbing courses at The National Mountaineering Centre, Plas-y-Brenin, Capel Curig, North Wales.

The Scottish Sports Council, Queensferry Street, Edinburgh runs courses at Glenmore Lodge Mountaineering Centre, Nr Aviemore.

Those are examples of available courses. There are many more, often run at mountain centres by local education authorities. Your own school, too, may offer climbing instruction on an informal basis where an experienced climber supervises groups of anybody interested. Sometimes climbing is on the curriculum at schools these days.

There are also climbing schools advertised in climbing magazines. Run by expert climbers, they provide bed, board and climbing instruction among the mountains and on the best climbs which all 'hard men' have done at some time.

How do you tell an ace 'hard man'? Often the backs of his hands will be cut and scarred – the result of jamming them into countless vertical rock face cracks.

Climbing clubs

Write to the British Mountaineering Council (BMC, Crawford House, Precinct Centre, Booth Street, East, Manchester), for details of the nearest climbing club. Even then a new club may recently have been started in your home town which is not on their list. So ask at the public library too. And enquire at the climbing shop serving your local area. You may live in the heart of East Anglia or other flat country, but there will still be a climbing club in the region somewhere. Often it will welcome new members – and beginners at that. Write to the secretary, say you are a novice, keen and can beginners join? You will probably be invited along on a weekend or evening meet. The rest is up to you.

YOUR FIRST ROCK CLIMB

Your first 'route' with a good climber leading the way will be carried out to the same sequence as you followed in Chapter 5 among the trees. You will still be climbing second man. You can use your bouldering gear too in fine weather on any crag near the road. . . .

You slog up the rocky path to the foot of the crag and each tie to the opposite ends of the climbing rope with a bowline or figure of eight. The climber starts up a slab so smooth the sweat from his fingers rolls down it after you have belayed to the rock pedestal. He stops at a good stance 30 feet above. 'Come on!' he shouts when he is ready. You yell, 'Climbing!', and your fingers go white as they cling to the tiny rock crystals which seem to be the only hand grips. A foot slips, but the rope catches you immediately. You grab back at handholds and start to climb as you did during practise. And now you begin to see how the rock is, in fact, weathered, scarred, wrinkled, riven and pitted into footholds and handholds – often as numerous as the holes in wire netting. You quickly reach the first stance without being pulled on the rope. 'That's O.K.' says your leader.

You belay to a spike as big as a cricket bat, put the rope around your back and, when the leader has undone his belay knot, pay out the rope once more as he tackles the next pitch. And now you begin to learn other tactics too. . . .

ROCK FACE BELAYING

The belaying principles in Chapter 5 done walking from tree to tree are now put to use on the crag. The leader shows you how to choose the safest belays – obvious on easy climbs where flakes, spikes, brackets, spillikins, bollards, horns, chockstones and other rock anchors now take the place of the trees you used in the park or a field.

Belaying with the rope

Check that the climbing rope runs right over rock anchors and cannot be accidentally disturbed. If it seems the rope may roll or skid off a rounded rock bollard – and there is no better anchor – slump down on the belay to lessen the chances of this happening. You may need to sit on the stance even. It pays to choose an anchor much higher than your waistline for this reason. And do secure the belay knot so that the rope comes down tight from the anchor to your waist. Always test spikes and flakes, too, by slapping them with the flat of your hand to see if they sound cracked or loose. Tug them hard – and chockstones too. If they move, or if in any doubt, look for another belay, and belay with slings and karabiners as well as the main rope to different parts of the rock above the stance where different anchors – often small – are available.

Belaying with slings, nuts and karabiners

Again, the ways you practise using a sling and karabiner as belays among trees can now be used on the crag. But your leader will carry the slings, and quite a number of them too. He will also have metal chocks or 'nuts' – mentioned in Chapter 2 – threaded on them, and you will have ample time to study how he uses them time and again as we shall see.

Rock face anchors can be used much more quickly when you belay with slings. Also, you discover many natural anchors too small for the thick climbing rope. So, instead, pass a sling over and round the spike or chockstone, sometimes doubled, then, clipping the doubled sling together with a karabiner, you snap the karabiner to your waistline – karabiner gate facing down.

You will come to use slings a great deal on climbs, but do remember their limitations. They are weaker than the thicker main rope – often being much thinner gauge rope or slender nylon webbing. And a karabiner might fail under the stress of a falling leader. On easy climbs belay with the main rope where possible, and when you use slings – use more than one sling.

An important point too: when belaying with a sling looped over a rock spike, first slide the metal chock into the centre of the sling – so the sling runs through the two holes in the metal without a kink. Forget to do this, and the sling then takes a 'U' bend through the two holes of the chock and is considerably weakened as a result.

Running belays

The leader will use a number of runners on each pitch – as practised in Chapter 5. After attaching each sling – the number can vary on a pitch from a couple to a dozen or more – he clips his rope through the karabiner and presses on. The smallest spikes, flakes, leafs and chockstones as big as tiny Meccano nuts can be used for slings as thin as bootlaces, especially on hard routes. These slender slings can snap during a leader's fall, of course, but they slow him down so that he is all the more readily stopped by the next big sling runner. On an easy pitch a leader will find good flakes, spikes and chockstones for his runners, but on harder climbs many of the runners are suspended from cracks – the leader inserts nuts into them carefully so that the slings hang down from the metal chocks wedged securely in these crevices (more on this a little later).

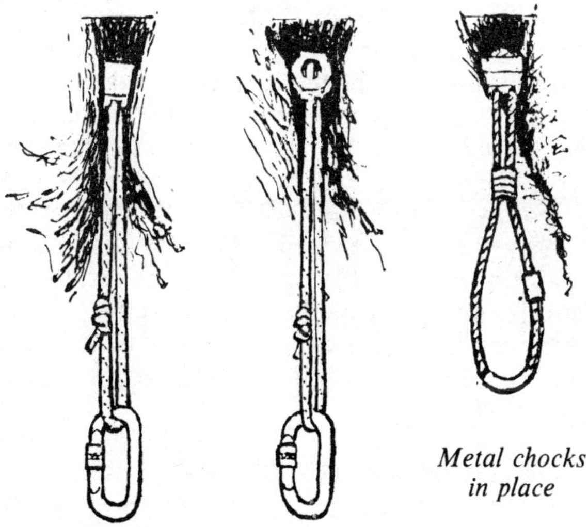

Metal chocks in place

Bringing up runners

As second – as in Chapter 5 – you will have to retrieve all the runners so you can hand them to the leader on his stance above. To free nuts jammed too securely carry an old table knife blade in a pocket after removing its handle with a hammer.

TWO REMINDERS REGARDING RUNNING BELAYS

If the leader tumbles on to a running belay, the second must be ready for a vicious pull upward which could lift him clear off his feet as the leader's weight hits the runner. Arrange stances and belays with this in mind, therefore, and for another good reason too – not only might you be hauled up from the stance, but you could also let go of the rope around your waist as a result. The slack rope would then unwind in seconds reeling you out to the bottom of the crag. So take extra care belaying. You need an anchor which will hold you down against such a pull – a chockstone is the ideal as it will hold you on the stance whatever the direction the pull of a falling leader comes from. But if only a spike belay is available, look also for an extra anchor like an undercut spike or crack where you might wedge a nut low down to keep your feet on the ledge whatever happens.

Secondly . . . Watch your leader for your own good in case he fails to place a runner at the top of a steep section before he then traverses across the face, say, to the right. If he forgets you could then be in for a hard time because by the time he reaches his stance at the end of the traverse, the rope is then stretching diagonally down across the face from the right rather than coming straight down the steep rock from above. And if you were to fall on this initial steep section the result would be a pendulum-like swing across the crag – and the possibility you will find it hard to get back on to the route. Would a leader mind your mentioning this? Good natured abuse flows freely on crags – so tell him.

ON YOUR OWN—FIRST STEPS

Never make the mistake of thinking you know it all after tackling several climbs behind a leader – even if he has let you lead on occasion. You simply don't know – it is true of any sport – how your performance will vary from day to day as a novice, nor how conditions will affect that performance. A climb you found straightforward on a sunny day could become a desperate struggle if you tried to repeat it in wind and rain. Do have some faith in your common senses, however. Young people can hurt themselves climbing trees. Few do. Not because there are regulations pinned up on every trunk, but because we generally have an instinctive knowledge of how far we can go. Trust to this and don't force it.

The equipment needed now

Once you start out on your own you need to spend on certain

items. The cost can be shared between partners. You need a climber's rucksack; crash hat, rock boots, 150 feet of 11mm kernmantel – you will probably go for kernmantel rope as it is more popular than hawser-laid rope; and about eight slings made up from nylon rope and webbing which you hang around your neck – each sling being threaded with a hexagonal or wedge-shaped nut as shown, and also attached to a karabiner. This may seem scant equipment, but the idea is that you add the extra accessories as you gain experience and gradually work up to harder climbs. Extra slings, nuts and karabiners, a climbing belt or harness, a descendeur and the rest are then obtained as and when you need them. Also, having too much paraphinalia at the beginning encourages the tyro to try tougher routes than he can really manage safely, and he comes to depend too much on the gear rather than on skill. For now, however, you can start by putting your rope to good use and practising further basics at home.

Coiling the rope

Always uncoil the rope coil by coil before using it. It avoids tangles. To coil, follow the diagram.

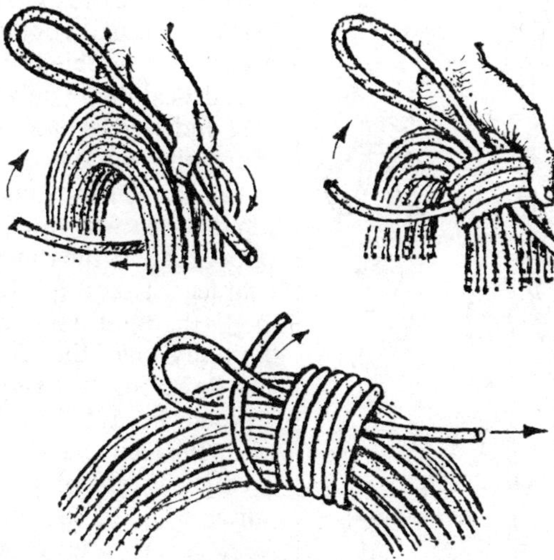

Going up and down the rope

These techniques where the rope is actually used as a handhold are essential to the climber. They can only be practised with a proper climbing rope, and then in safe settings of a grass slope for abseiling and a tree branch within a dozen feet from the ground for prusiking.

UP THE ROPE

Prusiking is a method of climbing up a climbing rope using prusik knots which can be slid along a rope when there is nothing pulling on them, but which will lock solid when a sudden weight is applied. Developed by a Viennese musician to mend his violin strings, the prusik knot has been adapted by climbers in a more advanced form too – the prusik devices as

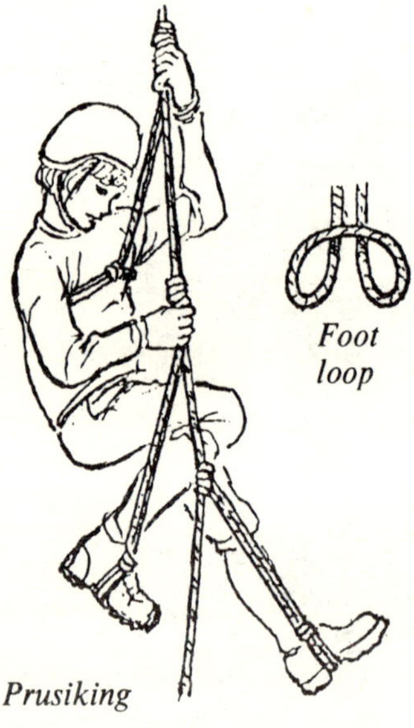

Prusiking

DOWN THE ROPE

Abseiling is the technique of sliding down a doubled rope – the second quickest way down a rock face. It lets you bale out from a climb which is proving too tough by 'abbing off' in a series of abseils back to the bottom. There are various abseil systems – the most popular today involving the use of the descendeur. But the basic abseils use ordinary gear, and you should practise these first.

Practise abseiling down a steep grass slope topped by a tree. (If you practise on low rocks, however, you must have a top rope – see prusiking.) Uncoil the rope, pass it round the tree, then coil it doubled. Throw the ends downhill as you would on a crag and see they are lying clear of any obstruction.

The *classic* abseil method is to stand as shown on top of the slope and pass the ropes between your legs. Take it round the right thigh (if right-handed), across the body, over the left shoulder and down into the right fist. To descend, hold the ropes in front with the left hand and walk backwards downhill. The friction is so good you will have to force your way down. Tips:

UP THE ROPE

used on peaks like Everest where climbers ascend fixed ropes using these clamps, like Jumars.

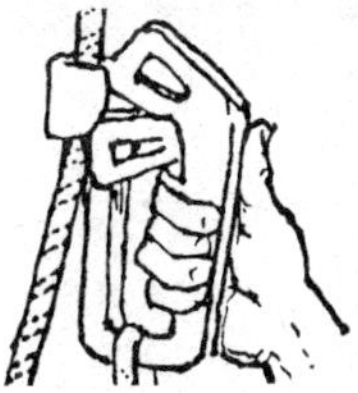

Mechanical prusik

The value in practising prusik now is: 1) you realise the rope's strength; 2) it gives you an intro to using prusiking devices on more advanced climbs; 3) it is a survival measure if you ever fall and end up spinning in mid-air spider-on-thread-fashion and your only escape is to climb back up the rope on prusik loops.

The illustration shows how with three short loops of 5/8in rope all tied with prusiks to a climbing rope hanging from a tree branch, you can climb up (and down) the dangling rope. Never try this on rock faces until you have mastered the technique – unless you are supervised and

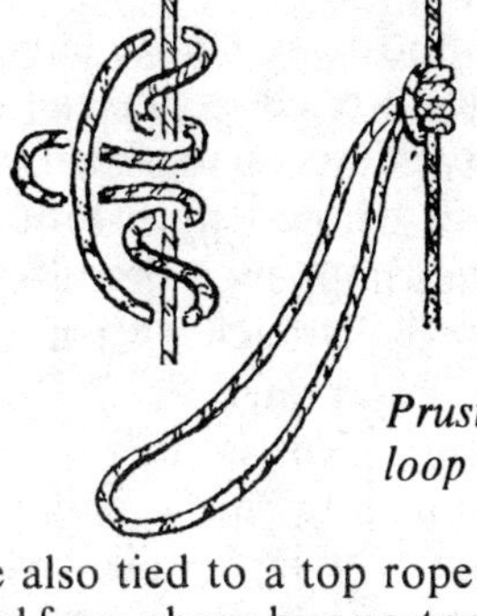

Prusik loop

are also tied to a top rope handled from above by a partner.

DOWN THE ROPE

don't grasp too hard with left hand. Brake with right hand by bringing it across into stomach. Lean right back, legs at 90° to slope. Pad in between legs and on shoulder.

Classic abseil

The *traditional* abseil uses a sling looped into a figure of eight in which you place a leg inside each loop, then pull it up to the crotch. Clip a screwgate karabiner on to the sling here, then clip abseil ropes into karabiner. Screw the gate up, pass the ropes over left shoulder and descend as shown. Don't try to speed and check no clothing can catch in the karabiner while sliding.

UP THE ROPE

Two tips. Experiment to find the right length of loops for most comfort. It depends on your build. To stop spinning around, weight the bottom of the rope with a sack full of stones as shown. Also: practise tying prusik knots one-handed as you might have to on a rock face.

Although prusiking and abseiling are automatic techniques, they are also the more potentially dangerous for this reason. You depend entirely on the rope and its anchor rather than on your own skill at staying suspended. As a result familiarity breeds contempt all the quicker – and a nasty accident happens. Many good climbers have died this way. Be careful.

DOWN THE ROPE

Traditional abseil

ABSEIL SAFETY CHECKLIST . . .

Anchor for rope MUST be solid (sound rock spike, chockstone or tree trunk). Check there are no crevices on anchor which could jam rope as when you have descended abseil it is necessary to pull one end of rope until whole length follows and if rope jams this is impossible (it has happened that abseil rope has jammed, and then climber prusiks back up rope to free it only for rope suddenly to come unjammed . . .). Rope must not be able to jump off spike either – ensure it is a *good* spike. If obvious rope will jam, place a sling round spike or chockstone, then double rope round this (you have to leave the sling in place, of course, but you are now safely down and can pull the rope through the sling without trouble). Always look down to check both ropes reach a reasonable ledge on a crag, or you could abseil off end of ropes. Starting an abseil is riskiest part when perched on brink of cliff and anchor for ropes is set low down. Where possible set up a safety rope with a companion safeguarding you – or vice-versa – during descent. Then, only last man down has to come unprotected, but previous abseilers have shown anchor and way are safe.

CHOOSING THE RIGHT CLIMBS

It is important at this stage that you avoid high mountain crags, although these do have splendid beginners' climbs. However, if you do slip or end up in a fix in bad weather you are vulnerable. Mountain rescue teams may be called out on your account, and no climber wants that. For the time being, aim for valley-bottom crags where the rock is near the road. But give limestone cliffs a miss in your early days. It is not good rock to start with – too friable by half. Keep to granite, gritstone or sandstone instead which make up the majority of crags anyway. Later you can do tremendous limestone climbs and, of course, go for those towering mountain fortresses too.

Reading the climbing guidebook

Guidebooks list all the routes which cover rock faces like the perpendicular and crossway spaces of a crossword puzzle. Borrow them from the public library, take them to bed and read them thoroughly. It takes time to understand what seems at first like a new language.

Since the 1860s climbers have pioneered climbs with names like *Needle Ridge, King Cobra, A Dream of White Horses, 'A' Route, Central Buttress, Cenotaph Corner* and *Kipling Groove*. These rock face routes are much bigger versions of boulder problems, and hundreds of feet high on many cliffs. They also include two big types of climb: *gullies* – like vertical wet, mossy canyons – which split a crag into *buttresses*, the great rock bastions in between gullies and on which are also found cracks, grooves, slabs, walls, overhangs and chimneys.

Rock climbs are graded as to difficulty: Easy, Moderate, Difficult, Very difficult, Severe, Very severe, Extremely severe. They are classified by number and size of holds, the quality of belays, the size of stances, the technical difficulty of the moves, the risk if the leader falls and so on. They are listed in the guidebook with entries like the one below.

> "Going up left across the scree a steep buttress is seen above large boulders. The climb goes up the light-coloured rock in the middle. YELLOW BRICK GROOVE. 150ft. Difficult. An interesting little climb on exposed rock.
>
> (1) 30ft. Climb the groove to a holly tree. Belay.
> (2) 40ft. Straight up the chimney, stepping right to pass a bulge. Thread belay.
> (3) 50ft. The crack is awkward to start. Holds then improve until a sentry box is reached. Belay.
> (4) 30ft. Pull strenuously over a wedged flake and climb the shallow corner leading to the top, and huge block belay."

Which crag?
You need a cliff with long easy routes rather than short tough climbs. Choose the crag which the guidebook describes as most popular (and near the road), where there is a wide range of climbing suitable for everyone – expert or novice. Check there are plenty of easies moderates and diffs too. A crag with only severes and VSs is no use yet.

Which routes?
Choose classics – the popular routes which have been climbed by thousands of previous climbers. Look through binoculars at any good crag from below and the classics become obvious because their holds are polished as clean as a thistle. But be careful. Great Gable's *Needle Ridge* is a classic v. diff.

The Needle
This is a 60ft rock tooth standing below which is also a classic and is 'only' graded v. diff – 'only' is in quotes because it is very much harder than the 300ft long *Needle Ridge*. Yet many are tempted on to the rock fang because of this apparently low grading – and they fail.

Be safe and work your way through the guidebook gradually. When you find the diffs no longer a problem, move on to the v. diffs and then severes. Stick to what the guidebook recommends as popular climbs and classics for now. A good thing about them: there is little chance of loose rock.

Spotting your route

Check the 'line' of your intended climb by reading the description carefully, and by checking the diagram of the crag where the climbs are laid out with dotted lines. This will help you find the start. On popular climbs the polished holds are an immediate indication. When a guidebook says 'A chimney on the right' it means when you are facing the rock. Popular climbs also mean there is often someone to ask – on a neighbouring climb or on the ground – when in doubt. 'Does *Vendetta* go up here, mate?'

Keeping on route

Again, ask if you're not sure. 'Am I right here?' You may have strayed from *Christmas Slab* – a diff – on to *Captain Fantastic* – a VS, and no wonder you are in danger of falling off. Refer to the diagram when in trouble. If you are on a popular easy climb where the holds are not clean and polished you are almost certainly off-route. Don't be fooled by the well-scratched wall, either, which proves unclimable – the boot marks have been caused by people abseiling down.

WHO LEADS NOW—AND HOW

Who leads where there are two inexperienced climbers on one rope? The one who performs best and finds leading comes most naturally on the boulder problems at home. If, however, you both discover climbing on the 'sharp end' – leading – is more fun than climbing second, you can both 'lead through'. This means your friend, say, leads the first pitch, you lead the second pitch, and he goes on to lead the third and so on. Some people take to leading at once, while others prefer climbing second all the time. It's also common to find leaders who specialise in certain pitches like cracks and grooves, say, but leave slabs and walls to their partner.

The leader's attitude

Try not to make a habit of top-roping climbs up low cliffs

where one of you can walk round to the top, belay, then drop the rope down so the other can climb second as it were up such and such a route. Learn by actually leading your way from the very easy to the harder climbs. (Top-roping is traditional technique on certain cliffs; normally, though, forget it.)

Safety-first precautions

Look on falling as all bad. Don't be misled by the hardest climbers – 'hard men' – who occasionally part company with the rock. They are protected by many slings and nuts, and competent seconds who know how to hold a fall, and they are still safer than you. Play safe by . . .

Always re-checking the guidebook to ensure the climb *is* easy and within your capabilities. (Make your limit diffs at first.)

HAVING THE BEST MAN LEAD

WEARING CLIMBING HELMETS

TAKING ALL THE BELAYING PRECAUTIONS. Namely: (1) Use the main rope to belay where possible on early climbs; (2) Use as thick a sling as possible when must; (3) Use several slings when anchors are small; always fix the sling tight and coming down to your waistline; have your belay rope coming down – to repeat it – to your waist.

Climbing slowly – and try not to rush because you feel everybody is watching you. Slow is normal on a crag.

Thinking about reversing each move upward you make.

Using runners whenever you have the chance . . . Especially after taking time off in a wood or below a local rock face or boulders and practising how to place nuts on slings into narrow rock cracks or tree trunks growing close together – as you stand on the ground. Push, wedge, jam, fiddle and poke them carefully into place just above where a crack narrows as shown. Tug down gently at first on the sling – with practise you can tell when a metal chock is really safely wedged and can hold a fall. Retrieving your metal nuts should be practised by levering with a metal comb or the knife blade previously mentioned. (You can, in fact, try this now – with conkers. Jam a conker in between the vertical cracks where tree trunks grow from the same bole or in cracks seaming thick, cracked bark on big trees. Tug downwards on the string and see if anyone can –

by pulling down – dislodge the conker. Conker or string will break first if you had jammed such a make-do 'nut' correctly.)

Resting below runners with the rope now coming down to you lets you take a breather.

Bale out from a runner if the climbing proves too hard – something you can nearly always do. Of course, you have to sacrifice the sling and karabiner unless you can flick it off the spike once you are safely down, but at least you are safe. It's also a lesson in not being over-keen to do harder climbs before you are ready.

OVERESTIMATE

Climbing rocks is all about getting up climbs. That is the nitty gritty of the sport. So long as you have taken all precautions, expect what climbers call an 'epic'. And that it will prove – again a climbing term – 'gripping'. It's a good thing to feel nervous beforehand, and shows your mind is turned in for problems ahead – from a knee-bending move you can't quite make to a foot that suddenly shoots off.

Be prepared to change your plans if it is wet and cold. Go for an easier climb in such cases. A diff, say, if you have been climbing v. diffs. Sometimes the diff might prove much harder than you expected too. Also, if you find you are failing on climbs, you are making the basic error of trying ascents that are too difficult for you. Curb your ambition therefore and go back to making easier ascents. Then, confidence restored, gradually try the harder routes again.

Think. . . . if-we-can-really-crack-this-climb-it-will-be-great. This gees you up and it shows in your climbing. You find the best belays, handle the rope efficiently and boost your partner's climbing as well whether he is leading or you are bringing him up as second on a tricky pitch you have just led. 'Great, man, nice climbing.' Encouragement helps a lot. Particularly if you expected the worst, then find as the route unfolds you realise you are succeeding after all. In fact, you usually make it to the top without having to retreat from a runner. Your preparations were thorough. You had the right state of mind. Give it the finishing touch, then . . .

BE AGGRESSIVE

Never give in too easily on a climb. Take your time and wear it down. Take plenty of rests. Puzzle it out. And expect a point where you think, 'If I do the next couple of moves I will really be committed and unable to go up or back down.' Well, this is the crux. YET if the climb is at your standard and you had double-checked this first, you won't want to retreat after making the difficult moves. Rest a moment or two immediately after climbing them, and new holds will come into view. You may also spot a runner up there which you hadn't seen from below. You are now 'climbing'.

WINTER DAYDREAMS

Let rock climbing be your medium for now. Rock is always accessible, the routes are always available and cleaned and tested by thousands who have gone before you. Rock climbs let you become accustomed to exposure and climbing movements in relative safety. You learn to judge steepness, handle the rope and gain a sixth sense of where the danger lies when you climb every weekend and during summer evenings too. Snow and ice climbing is a different ball of wax, however. And one you should leave until you have gained experience on rock, and also made the acquaintance of other competent climbers to partner you on winter climbs – even the easy ones.

Winter conditions vary so enormously from day to day that the novice literally never really knows where he stands. Avalanche risks are always present, especially in Scotland; yes, even on relatively low peaks where ice-choked gullies give a fabulous lure to the greenhorn desperate to try out a new ice axe and crampons. And belay anchors are not reliable on snow and ice unless you are experienced. Do bide your time therefore. The winter climbing practised in Chapter 6 was designed for your own safety during winter hill walks, should you meet bad conditions along the path, rather than encouraging you to set out on steep snow and ice routes. And even this hill walking should be done in the company of a competent mountaineer.

Nothing sums up the unpredictable nature of snow and ice more than the cornice – the wing of hard frozen snow which is swept out over space from a skyline smothered in snow by the wind, and sculptured into place by the cold. This roof, so obvious from the mountainside below, is quite invisible from above and a climber – and good climbers have, and died – can stand on top and think he is treading the solid crest of the mountain. One moment he is on the very pinnacle of a glistening landscape, the next – without warning – he is falling through space as the snow gives beneath his boots. Such is danger of winter to the unwary. And this is why, when your time comes, to tackle winter climbs, the young climber finds all the more thrills in what is certainly *greater* mountaineering – as he becomes more and more at home on rock and snow and ice. Fantastic!

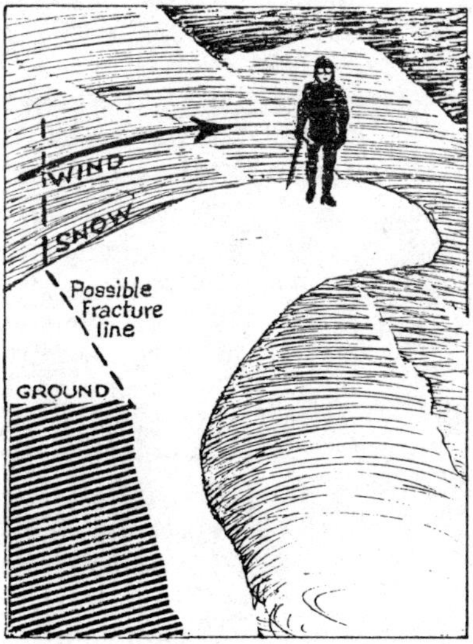

Index

Abseiling, 118, 120
Axe, ice 12, 13, 20, 91-102

Belaying, 71-90, 106-8, 113-6
Belts, 14, 16
Bivouac bag, 13
Boots, 10, 18, 25
Bouldering, 35-63
Breeches, climbing, 11
Bridging, 52

Cagoules, 11, 20
Chimneying, 51
Chocks, 15, 114
Compass, 26-7
Contours, 30
Contouring, 32
Crampons, 17, 91

Dead man, 17, 106-9
Descendeur, 16

Food rations, 12, 25
Footholds, 44

Gaiters, 11, 19
Glissading, 95
Gloves, 11, 20
Handholds, 45
Harness, 14
Helmet, crash 14, 21
Hypothermia, 24

Ice screws, 17

Jumars, 16

Karabiners, 16, 65-90, 107, 114
Knots, 65 *et seq.*,

Mantelshelfing, 55
Ordnance Survey maps, 12, 28-30
Pitons, 16
Prusiking, 118
Rope, 14, 64, 76-90
Rucksack, climbing 12, 20
Runners, 85-6, 115

Scree, 32
Shoes, rock climbing 10, 18
Slings, 14, 88, 114
Steps, cutting 100-4
Stockings, 11, 18
Sweaters, 11, 20

Torch, head- 12
Trousers, 11, 19

Walking hints, 22-30
Weather checks, 33-4